S. Hrg. 115–40, Pt. 1

DISINFORMATION: A PRIMER IN RUSSIAN ACTIVE MEASURES AND INFLUENCE CAMPAIGNS PANEL I

HEARING

BEFORE THE

SELECT COMMITTEE ON INTELLIGENCE

OF THE

UNITED STATES SENATE

ONE HUNDRED FIFTEENTH CONGRESS

FIRST SESSION

THURSDAY, MARCH 30, 2017

Printed for the use of the Select Committee on Intelligence

Available via the World Wide Web: http://www.fdsys.gov

U.S. GOVERNMENT PUBLISHING OFFICE

25–362 PDF   WASHINGTON : 2017

For sale by the Superintendent of Documents, U.S. Government Publishing Office
Internet: bookstore.gpo.gov Phone: toll free (866) 512–1800; DC area (202) 512–1800
Fax: (202) 512–2104 Mail: Stop IDCC, Washington, DC 20402–0001

CONTENTS

DISINFORMATION: A PRIMER IN RUSSIAN ACTIVE MEASURES AND INFLUENCE CAMPAIGNS
PANEL I

THURSDAY, MARCH 30, 2017

U.S. SENATE,
SELECT COMMITTEE ON INTELLIGENCE,
Washington, DC.

The Committee met, pursuant to notice, at 10:10 a.m. in Room SD–106, Dirksen Senate Office Building, Hon. Richard Burr (Chairman of the Committee) presiding.

Committee Members Present: Senators Burr, Warner, Risch, Rubio, Collins, Blunt, Lankford, Cotton, Cornyn, Feinstein, Wyden, Heinrich, King, Manchin, and Harris.

OPENING STATEMENT OF HON. RICHARD BURR, CHAIRMAN, A U.S. SENATOR FROM NORTH CAROLINA

Chairman BURR. I'd like to call this hearing to order. I apologize to our witnesses that we had a vote that was called at 10:00 and most members are in the process of making their way from there to here.

This morning the committee will engage in an activity that's quite rare for us, an open hearing on an ongoing critical intelligence question: the role of Russian active measures past and present. As many of you know, this committee is conducting a thorough, independent, and nonpartisan review of the Russian active measures campaign conducted against the 2016 U.S. elections.

Some of the intelligence provided to the committee is extremely sensitive, which requires that most of the work be conducted in a secure setting to maintain the integrity of the information and to protect the very sensitive sources and methods that gave us access to that intelligence. However, the Vice Chairman and I understand the gravity of the issues that we're here reviewing and have decided that it's crucial that we take the rare step of discussing publicly an ongoing intelligence question.

That's why we've convened this second open hearing on the topic of Russian active measures, and I can assure you to the extent possible the committee will hold additional open hearings on this issue.

The American public, indeed all democratic societies, need to understand that malign actors are using old techniques with new platforms to undermine our democratic institutions.

This hearing, entitled "Disinformation: A Primer in Russian Active Measures and Influence Campaigns," will consist of two panels and will provide a foundational understanding of Russian active measures and information operations campaigns. The first panel will examine the history and characteristics of those campaigns. The second panel will examine the history and characteristics of those campaigns and the role and capabilities of cyber operations in support of these activities.

Unfortunately, you will learn today that these efforts by Russia to discredit the U.S. and weaken the West are not new. These efforts are in fact a part of Russian, and previous Soviet Union, intelligence efforts. You will learn today that our community has been a target of Russian information warfare, propaganda, and cyber campaigns and still is.

The efforts our experts will outline today continue unabated. The takeaway from today's hearing: We're all targets of a sophisticated and capable adversary and we must engage in a whole-of-government approach to combat Russian active measures.

Today we'll receive testimony from experts who have in some cases worked directly to respond to active measures, who understand the history and the context of active measures, and whose significant experience and knowledge will shed new light on the problem and provide useful context. Doctors Godson and Rumer, Mr. Watts, we're grateful to you for your appearance here today.

This afternoon we will reconvene and welcome witnesses who will discuss the technical side of the question, cyber operations, including computer network exploitation, social media, and online propaganda activities, and how they enable and promote Russian influence campaigns and information operations.

We have a full day ahead of us and I'm confident that the testimony you will hear today will help you to establish a foundational understanding of the problem as the committee continues its inquiry into Russian activities.

Finally, I'd like to commend the Vice Chairman for his dedication to the goals of the committee's inquiry and to the integrity of the process. The Vice Chairman and I realize that if we politicize this process our efforts will likely fail. The public deserves to hear the truth about possible Russian involvement in our elections, how they came to be involved, how we may have failed to prevent that involvement, what actions were taken in response, if any, and what we plan to do to ensure the integrity of future free elections at the heart of our democracy.

Gentlemen, thank you again for your willingness to be here, and I turn to the Vice Chairman.

OPENING STATEMENT OF HON. MARK R. WARNER, VICE CHAIRMAN, A U.S. SENATOR FROM VIRGINIA

Vice Chairman WARNER. Thank you, Mr. Chairman. I also want to welcome our witnesses today.

Today's hearing is important to help understand the role Russia played in the 2016 presidential elections. As the U.S. intelligence community unanimously assessed in January of this year, Russia sought to hijack our democratic process, and that most important part of our democratic process, our presidential elections.

As we'll learn today, Russia's strategy and tactics are not new, but their brazenness certainly was. The hearing is also important because it's open, as the Chairman mentioned, which is sometimes unusual for this committee. Due to the classified nature of our work, we typically work behind closed doors.

Today's public hearing will help, I hope, the American public writ large understand how the Kremlin made effective use of its hacking skills to steal and weaponize information and engage in a coordinated effort to damage a particular candidate and to undermine public confidence in our democratic process.

Our witnesses today will help us to understand how Russia deployed this deluge of disinformation in a broader attempt to undermine America's strength and leadership throughout the world.

We simply must and we will get this right. The Chairman and I agree it is vitally important that we do this in as credible, bipartisan, and transparent manner as possible. As we said yesterday at our press conference, Chairman Burr and I trust each other and, equally important, we trust our colleagues on this committee, that we are going to move together and we're going to get to the bottom of this and do it right.

As this hearing begins, let's take just one moment to review what we already know. Russia's President, Vladimir Putin, ordered a deliberate campaign carefully constructed to undermine our election. First Russia struck at our political institutions by electronically breaking into the headquarters of one of our political parties and stealing vast amounts of information. Russian operatives also hacked emails to steal personal messages and other information from individuals ranging from Clinton Campaign Manager John Podesta to former Secretary of State Colin Powell.

This stolen information was then weaponized. We know that Russian intelligence used the quote-unquote Guccifer 2 persona and others like WikiLeaks at seemingly choreographed times that would cause maximum damage to one candidate.

They did this with an unprecedented level of sophistication about American presidential politics that should be a line of inquiry for us on this committee and, candidly, while it helped one candidate this time, they are not favoring one party over another and consequently it should be a concern for all of us.

Second, Russia continually sought to diminish and undermine our trust in the American media by blurring our faith in what is true and what is not. Russian propaganda outlets like RT and Sputnik successfully produced and peddled disinformation to American audiences in pursuit of Moscow's preferred outcome. This Russian propaganda on steroids was designed to poison the national conversation in America.

The Russians employed thousands of paid internet trolls and botnets to push out disinformation and fake news at a high volume, focusing this material onto your Twitter and Facebook feeds and flooding our social media with misinformation. This fake news and disinformation was then hyped by the American media echo chamber and our own social media networks to reach and potentially influence millions of Americans.

This is not innuendo or false allegations. This is not fake news. This is actually what happened to us. Russia continues these sorts of actions as we speak. Some of our close allies in Europe are experiencing exactly the same kind of interference in their political process. Germany has said that its parliament has been hacked. French presidential candidates right now have been the subject of Russian propaganda and disinformation. In The Netherlands, their recent election, the Dutch hand-counted their ballots because they feared Russian interference in their electoral process. Perhaps most critically for us, there is nothing to stop them from doing this all over again in 2018 for those of you who are up or in 2020 as Americans again go back to the polls.

In addition to what we already know, any full accounting must also find out what, if any, contacts, communications, or connections occurred between Russia and those associated with the campaigns themselves. I will not prejudge the outcome of our investigation. We are seeking to determine if there is an actual fire, but there is clearly a lot of smoke.

For instance, an individual associated with the Trump campaign accurately predicted the release of hacked emails weeks before it happened. This same individual also admits to being in contact with Guccifer 2, the Russian intelligence persona responsible for these cyber operations.

The platform of one of our two major political parties was mysteriously watered down in a way which promoted the interests of President Putin and no one seems to be able to identify who directed that change in the platform.

The campaign manager of one campaign who played such a critical role in electing the President was forced to step down over his alleged ties to Russia and its associates.

Since the election, we've seen the President's National Security Adviser resign and his Attorney General recuse himself over previously undisclosed contacts with the Russian government.

And of course, in the other body on March 20th the Director of the FBI publicly acknowledged that the Bureau was, quote, "investigating the nature of any links between individuals associated with the Trump campaign and the Russian government and whether there was any coordination between the campaign and Russian efforts." End of quote.

I want to make clear, at least for me, this investigation is not about whether you have a "D" or an "R" next to your name. It is not about relitigating last fall's election. It is about clearly understanding and responding to this very real threat. It's also, I believe, about holding Russia accountable for this unprecedented attack on our democracy. And it is about arming ourselves so we can identify and stop it when it happens again. And trust me, it will happen again if we don't take action.

I would hope that the President is as anxious as we are to get to the bottom of what happened. But I have to say editorially that the President's recent conduct, with his wild and uncorroborated accusations about wiretapping and his inappropriate and unjustified attacks on America's hardworking intelligence professionals does give me grave concern.

This committee has a heavy weight of responsibility to prove that we can continue to put our political labels aside to get us to the truth. I believe we can get there. I've seen firsthand—and I say this to our audience—how serious members on both sides of this dais have worked on this sensitive and critical issue.

As the Chairman and I have said repeatedly, this investigation will follow the facts where they lead us. If at any time I believe we're not going to be able to get those facts—and we're working together very cooperatively to make sure we get the facts that we need from the intelligence community. We will get that done.

Mr. Chairman, again I thank you for your commitment to the serious work and your commitment to keeping this bipartisan cooperation at least, if not all across the Hill, alive in this committee. Thank you very much.

Chairman BURR. I thank the Vice Chairman.

Members should note that they will be recognized by seniority for five-minute questions. We'll go as expeditiously as we can.

Let me introduce our witnesses today if I may and we will hear from those witnesses: Dr. Roy Godson, Emeritus Professor of Government, Georgetown University. Dr. Godson has specialized in security studies and international relations at Georgetown University for more than four decades. Thank you for that.

As a scholar, he helped pioneer intelligence studies in American higher education, editing the seven-volume series "Intelligence Requirements for the 1980s, 1990s," and co-founding the Consortium for Study of Intelligence. He's directed, managed, and published with other scholars and practitioners "Innovative Studies on Adapting American Security Paradigms," "Intelligence Dominance Consistent with Rule of Law Practices," and "Strategies for Preventing and Countering Global Organized Crime."

Dr. Godson has served as consultant to the United States Security Council, the President's Foreign Intelligence Advisory Board, and related agencies of the U.S. Government.

Thank you for your service and thank you for being here.

Dr. Rumer is a Senior Fellow and Director of the Russian and Eurasian Program, Carnegie Endowment for International Peace. Prior to joining Carnegie, Dr. Rumer served as the National Intelligence Officer for Russia and Eurasia at the U.S. National Intelligence Council from 2010 to 2014. Earlier he held research appointments at the National Defense University, the International Institute for Strategic Studies, and the Rand Corporation.

He has served on the National Security Council staff and at the State Department, taught at Georgetown University and George Washington University, and published widely.

Welcome, Dr. Rumer.

Clint Watts. Clint Watts is a Robert Fox Fellow for the Foreign Policy Research Institute and a Senior Fellow at the Center for Cyber and Homeland Security at George Washington University. Clint is a consultant and researcher modeling and forecasting threat actor behavior and developing countermeasures for disrupting and defeating state and non-state actors.

As a consultant, Clint designs and implements customized training and research programs for military, intelligence, and law enforcement organizations at the Federal, State, and local levels. Clint served as a United States Army infantry officer, an FBI agent on a joint terrorism task force, as the executive officer of the Combatting Terrorism Center at West Point, and as a consultant to the FBI's Counterterrorism Division and National Security Branch.

Clinton, welcome. Thank you for your service.

With that, I will recognize our witnesses from my left to right. Dr. Godson, you are recognized.

STATEMENT OF ROY GODSON, Ph.D., EMERITUS PROFESSOR OF GOVERNMENT, GEORGETOWN UNIVERSITY

Dr. GODSON. Thank you, Mr. Chairman and Vice Chairman and members of the committee, for inviting me to this hearing. I'd like to begin with just a minute or two on the long history of Soviet active measures and then talk a little bit about some of the major advantages the Soviets and the Russians have reaped from their history of using this instrument. Finally, I'd like to come to what we have done in the past to reduce the effectiveness of Soviet behavior and what we might want to consider for the future.

I think if one looks at the history of the last 100 years you're going to find that the Russians and their Soviet predecessors have believed that active measures is a major tool for their advancement. They actually believe, whatever we think about it, that this gives them the possibility of achieving influence well beyond their economic and social status and conditions in their country.

I think when you look at what they say now, what they do now, and the way they act and practice and talk about their active measures, they take this subject very seriously.

Sometimes we in the United States have been aware of this, but for many, many decades we did not take this subject seriously and they were able to take enormous advantage. I think today that they basically believe they can use these techniques rather similarly to many of the ways they did this in the past. I do think that they are repeating many of the same practices that they did in the past. Yes, there may be some new techniques that are being used now. In fact there are, and some of my colleagues on the panel and this afternoon are more expert on those techniques, particularly the use of the internet and particularly cyberspace.

But we can more or less rest assured that the Soviets will be looking at other techniques and will be seeking to adapt and make their active measures much more productive for them in the future.

Yes, the activities in the United States that you're particularly interested in do seem to be exceptional. We don't have very many other examples of where they interfered with election machinery and electoral apparatuses. What we do have are many, many examples of where the Soviets, working together, were able, with their allies abroad, their agents of influence abroad, to actually affect the elections in many, many countries in the 20th and early 21st centuries.

The Soviets and their Russian successors took the view, take the view, that they are able to hit above their weight, they can fight above their weight, if they use active measures. They don't want to go to war. Neither of us wants to go to war. But they take the view that they can actually achieve a lot of what they want to do through their active measures. That is, the combination of overt and covert techniques and resources, overt and covert combined together in one pattern, and that they have the authority and the responsibility as leaders of the country to be able to do that. And they put this into practice.

In the 1920s and 1930s they created an enormous apparatus in the world. Russia was a poor, weak country and yet Russia in the 1920s and 1930s set up whole organizations, overt and covert, throughout the world that were able to challenge all the major powers of Europe and the United States. We may not have realized that these organizations were being set up, but they were considerable, and it took a lot of effort and skill on their part to do this.

In the war, the Second World War, they used this apparatus to be able to influence the politics of Europe after the war. Yes, they also used it during the war to help them, and sometimes us, in fighting the Nazis and the Italian fascists. But in a major way they were also preparing for being able to influence the outcome of the struggle for the balance of power in Europe during World War II. So while they were an ally, they were also planning to undermine democratic and liberal parties, including in the United States at that time.

In fact, they were able to take advantage of the fact that we were friendly and that we were working together. Uncle Joe was a friend of the United States at that time, they thought, and they were able to use that very successfully. So as a result, they were nearly able to take over the balance of power in Western Europe. It was a closely run contest, and of course we're all glad that they lost. But it was a very closely run conflict and we did emerge successfully from it.

In the 1980s, they were on another roll. They used their apparat, which built up in, as I say, the 1920s and 1930s, 1940s, 1950s, and 1960s, to be able to achieve a great deal in the late 1970s and 1980s. They nearly were able to split Europe, split NATO in Europe, in the 1980s. They started that in the last year of the Carter Administration and continued into the Reagan years. Fortunately, we noticed this in time and our rearmament of NATO went ahead and it wasn't because the Soviets wanted it, but because we were able to outmaneuver them.

The 1990s were sort of chaotic there and so their active measures apparatus wasn't very effective and it didn't have the kind of leadership that it had had before and the kind of leadership it has gained since Vladimir Putin came to power. It's maybe a little bit too soon to do an assessment of their effectiveness. So far, as was pointed out earlier by the Chairman and the Vice Chairman, we do think that they were effective in an important way to us, and we understand that the committee is going to be looking into this and studying this.

But in any event, they have this apparatus. They have modernized it. They were spending billions of dollars a year before. They have maybe 10 to 15,000 people in this apparatus at least worldwide, in addition to the trolls and other kinds of cyber capabilities they have.

But the Soviets are not ten feet tall——

Chairman BURR. Dr. Godson, I'm going to interrupt you for just a second, just to make members aware that the second vote has started and it's our intent to work through this second vote. So I'd ask members as they feel comfortable to leave for the vote, come right back if you will. As soon as we get through the panel, we'll start questions.

Dr. Godson, I'd just ask you to summarize as quickly as you can.

Senator FEINSTEIN. Mr. Chairman, how long is a round?

Chairman BURR. Five-minute recognition.

Dr. GODSON. They're not ten feet tall. They have used their capabilities effectively, but they don't always win out.

The United States for the first time responded in a major way to them in the late 1940s through the 1960s. We did in fact cauterize their active measures apparatus and they were not able to successfully use it in Western Europe and other parts of the world. We did some things pretty well from the 1940s to the 1960s.

Unfortunately, in the 1960s the coalition between liberals and conservatives, the consensus between the Congress and the administration, started to fall apart. Then, with the criticisms that the intelligence community had to take in that time, our countermeasures started to fall apart and we were sort of disarming ourselves, if I can say that. So from the 1960s through the late 1970s we did not have a very effective counter-active measures capability and the Russians, of course, took advantage of that in numerous places in the world.

In the 1980s, though, that changed. In the late 1970s, 1980s, it changed and we did start to do things well again. I'll just summarize the fact that we started to develop a strategic approach to countermeasures. It wasn't a bit here and a bit there and so on. It was actually a strategic approach, with warning and anticipation of active measures. We actually would study them so well that we were able to often anticipate what they were going to do with active measures and so therefore we could then use other measures to limit them and avoid the effectiveness of these active measures.

We also started to support liberal elements abroad that we thought would be helpful to us in preventing Soviet active measures from furthering Soviet objectives in those societies.

So we were fairly successful in the 1980s in doing this and in both using overt and covert methods to do this. As in other victories that we've had after World War I or after World War II, after the Cold War we thought that this wasn't such an important thing to be doing any more and so our activities waned. They didn't stop, but they waned. We had some units that remained in the government that were concerned with this, but on the whole the government actually disarmed itself.

So although there were some in the government and outside the government who warned about the Soviet use of active measures—and I do know when looking over the website of your committee that some of the people in this room actually went to the government and asked the government to be more mindful of Soviet active measures starting in 2016, and presumably we should be mindful of it afterwards—unfortunately, the government did not take the warnings as seriously as it could have and made this known to the public in a useful fashion so we would not be so surprised when this took place in the—or appears to have taken place in 2016.

But the Soviets could not have done this and the Russians could not have done this without having an active measures apparatus.

It's visible. One can find it. One can't find everything about it, but we have—historically, we know that we can find it, we can anticipate it, and we can take a number of measures. So I hope you will have time to consider, maybe in the questioning, some of the measures we could now take to do that.

Thank you.

[The prepared statement of Dr. Godson follows:]

**Written Testimony of ROY GODSON to the
Senate Select Committee on Intelligence, Open Hearing, March 30, 2017
"Disinformation: A Primer in Russian Active Measures and Influence
Campaigns."**

Thank you Chairman Burr and Vice Chairman Warner for the opportunity to testify today on Russian Active Measures and Influence Campaigns.

My name is Roy Godson, and I am Emeritus Professor of Government at Georgetown University.

Active Measures (AM) have been a significant weapon in the Russian and Soviet arsenal for over 100 years. By active measures is meant the coordinated direction by the centralized authoritarian hierarchy of a combination of overt and covert techniques that propagate Russian, (formerly Soviet) ideas, political/military preferences and undermine those of their democratic adversaries. Disinformation – intentionally disseminating false information such as forgeries - is just one of the many overt and covert influence techniques used by the Russian/Soviet leadership in what they call "active measures."[1] A more comprehensive definition is offered at the end of this statement.

There is little new in the basic mindset of successive generations of Russian leadership. These influence techniques provide their relatively weak economy and insecure political institutions with a strategic and tactical advantage to affect significant political outcomes abroad. *They say so. They do it.* But they are not ten feet tall. They build up skilled, experienced, and tenacious teams at home in their government and quasi-government agencies. They maintain and develop both an overt and covert apparatus of well-trained personnel to continue their manipulation of foreign agents of influence, and use new geotechnologies that come online as force enhancers. Some of it is effective, some just a nuisance.

---

[1] For a brief listing of major active measures techniques, See, Richard Shultz and Roy Godson, *Dezinformatsia: Active Measures in Soviet Strategy*, Pergamon-Brassey's, 1984.

In the final years of the Soviet Union there was enough information on their active measures systems to conclude that approximately 15,000 personnel and several billions of hard currency annually were being spent on these activities— aimed mostly at the U.S. and its allies.

Yet even with knowledge of these activities and their long-term training of personnel, as well as studies by Western scholars, information from former Soviet defectors in the active measures "industry," the attentive public and most elected officials still continue to be surprised by Russia's operational behavior.

Recent events are not the first time we have been SURPRISED.

Punching Above Their Weight

After World War I, a few Americans and others had warned about these "below the radar" threats. Some were veterans of the internecine wars during and after the Bolshevik Revolution and were aware of the Communist "ways" of politics. They also reported that Lenin and Stalin had already started to build up the capability—since encompassed by the term "Active Measures"—in the Twenties to defend the Revolution and to influence world politics. The Soviet Politburo and the Party departments directed, controlled, and financed active measures and serviced them through the Soviet intelligence system and Soviet diplomacy, These instruments and capability provided influence throughout the world to the economically weak Soviet regime along with its faithful allies inside most of the democratic (and illiberal) societies—from the 1930s to the early 1990s.

Moscow reinforced its sway by creating and controlling an apparently independent mostly overt grouping of the Communist parties known as the Communist International. This International, in turn, was bolstered by another set of organized national and international Front groups, again apparently independent of Soviet control. These "nongovernmental" Fronts were designed to appeal to non-communists and political activists who were attracted or amenable to Soviet views in specific sectors such as "labor," "youth," "peace," "religion," and "culture." The Parties and Fronts changed their views and their tactics in response to Moscow's direction, working, for example, against the Nazi and Fascist rise to power in Europe in the 1930s until 1939.

Then, after the Hitler-Stalin Non-Aggression Pact in 1939, which divided Poland in two and enabled Moscow to consolidate control the Baltic States, Stalin switched policies. No longer did Communists parties and fronts work against the Nazis. Instead they condemned "capitalist liberals" and sought to influence and undermine the political system in the West. Stalinist policy flipped again when Germany attacked Russia in 1941, and for the rest of the war the Russians mobilized the Communist parties and the Fronts to support the Soviet Union in the war effort and take over the then anti-Nazi Resistance in Europe.

They used this Resistance role to gain spectacular influence in postwar European politics, particularly in France and Italy, and almost in West Germany as well as in Britain and other countries. The Communist Parties and fronts also helped – overtly and covertly- in recruiting agents of influence, and some Western leaders and voters, who had become sympathetic to the anti-Nazi and Fascist positions of the Soviet Union, and the peace movements and other issue organizations that the Soviets significantly influenced. An extensive academic, journalistic, and biographic literature is now available on these efforts.[2]

Little evidence has come to the fore of Soviet direct meddling in the actual mechanical election processes of major countries; but they did try to influence the outcomes of the elections and the behavior of foreign leaders in parties, trade unions, the media, and culture. Sometimes they were successful, sometimes less so. While leaders of democratic governments came to be generally aware of Soviet influence attempts, they rarely attracted the ire and response of the United States until later. Nevertheless, using their broad active measures capability, in the post WWII context, the Soviets almost succeeded in shifting the entire postwar political balance of power in Western Europe.

A Closely Fought Battle

This strategic capability went almost unnoticed during WWII and the first years afterwards. But gradually, the scope of long-term Soviet penetration and active measures in Europe, and the United States, came into focus – and to public attention. The battle for political power in post-

---

[2] See for example, Haynes, John Earl, Harvey Klehr, and Alexander Vassiliev. 2010. *Spies: The Rise and Fall of the KGB in America*. Yale University Press. See also, Godson, Roy, *American Labor and European Politics, The AFL as Transnational Force*, Crane, Russak, 1976. Shultz and Godson, *Dezinformatsia*.

war Western Europe – then the pivot of world politics – galvanized U.S. action at home and abroad. It was a formidable response.

The Truman and Eisenhower administrations developed a national "whole of government" and "whole of society" political strategy to neutralize Soviet active measures from the late 1940s on. This was a calculation to partially complement both U.S. foreign economic policy (e.g. The Marshall Plan) and its military strategy (e.g. NATO). Initially, there was a good deal of improvisation. Gradually, however the bipartisan political leadership, the Executive Branch, and Congress, together with the support of the private sector, labor, and philanthropy, and education were awakened to the threat and mobilized in support. There were, of course, American mistakes, and some demagoguery – especially in the early 1950s from Senator Joseph McCarthy and his team who exploited public concern, exaggerated the danger, and overreacted.

Yes, from the late 1940s forward the U.S. and other liberal democracies did use overt and covert measures to defend and assist democratic elements abroad—labor, media, intellectuals, and parties—that were under direct attack abroad by well-trained and financed political forces from the Soviet Bloc.

By the late 1960s the political consensus in the U.S. and to some extent among democratic allies abroad began to fray, particularly during the Vietnam War. The coalition of American liberals and conservatives against Soviet active measures came apart. Congressional criticism of the intelligence community and the dismantling of much of the U.S. capability to counter Active Measures abroad also contributed.

Also in the 1970s, the Nixon Administration began to seek "Détente" with the USSR and that too diminished government support for exposing and criticizing Soviet active measures abroad. By the advent of the Carter Administration in the mid-1970s, interest in and the ability to counter Soviet influence operations abroad had waned substantially.

That changed when we were "surprised" again —this time by the Soviet invasion of its neighbor Afghanistan, Soviet support for Cuban expeditions in Africa, the Sandinista takeover of Nicaragua and the threat to El Salvador. This was intensified by the Soviet build-up of warfighting capabilities aimed at Western Europe and vigorous Soviet active measures campaigns there – with the goal of minimizing the NATO response.[3] Even before Reagan took office in 1981 awareness of the importance of a response was growing in Washington.

Fortunately, U.S. government capabilities had not been entirely dismantled in the 1970s. There were still a few veteran specialists in the USG – State, CIA, DOD, DIA, and the then USIA, as well as some in Congress – who had maintained a watching brief on the issues. They were complemented by American NGOs such as the mainstream of organized labor and key philanthropic and human rights organizations who had sustained attention and enquiry on Soviet active measures. Once again, plans to counter Soviet Active Measures were reprised, first with educational campaigns and then with significant tangible support to democratic elements at home and abroad.

After a brief interlude in the Yeltsin years of the 1990s and the demise of both the Soviet Communist Party and its ideology of Marxism Leninism, the regime regrouped this time under the leadership of Vladimir Putin. He came to power together with a coterie of former colleagues, many also trained in the Soviet security and intelligence system. They no longer had a competitive global ideology, and much of their widespread apparatus such as Communist Parties and Front groups was not particularly useful. What they did share with their predecessors was an animosity toward liberal democracy.

They were and are determined to achieve most of the same objectives as the Soviet Communist Party leadership had had before them. As determined Russian nationalists they sought power and influence, and, of course, discrediting the U.S. and democratic society in general. Their focus is almost completely negative, zeroing in on creating chaos and division in what has been called an "age of anger" in many parts of the world.[4] This opens up many opportunities for influence.

Their active measures apparatus appears to still recruit and train operatives for the global context. They identify and pursue opportunities as they see them. They still use a combination (Kombinatsia) of overt and covert techniques that date back to Czarist days to reinforce their medium to long-term objectives. Of course, they have taken advantage of the new advances in

---

[3] Godson Roy, *Dirty Tricks or Trump Cards: U.S. Covert Action and Counterintelligence*, Transaction, 2000.
[4] Mishra, Pankaj. *Age of Anger: A History of the Present*. New York: Farrar, Straus and Giroux, 2017. See also Friedman Thomas L. *Thank You for Being Late:An Optimist's Guide to Thriving in the Age of Accelerations*, Farrar, Straus and Giroux, 2016

global technologies, most notably the Internet and new media[5] – and are also likely pursuing other geotechnologies coming on stream soon.[6]

As one student of the subject has put it, "they are mixing old and new wine in new bottles — but the distributor is basically the same."

The U.S. Response in the 1980s

The U.S. government began to develop a strategic approach to the problem by mobilizing an interagency effort in the early Reagan years. This difficult and complex task took time and effort. The various departments and agencies concerned with national security slowly began to pull together to provide details to the American people about Soviet activities designed to influence American and allied politics.

Achieving this synergy required that the President request and receive support from the Congress to authorize and fund more gathering of information from overt and intelligence sources about the specifics of Soviet AM, and to analyze and even to anticipate their likely future operations. It was reinforced by the creation of what came to be known as the interagency "Active Measures Working Group," based first in the State Department and later in the U.S. information Agency.[7] Some of the findings were used to educate Americans, Europeans, and others that Moscow was conducting major campaigns to discredit democracy in general, and the U.S. in particular,

As a result, countering Soviet active measures became a government concern and an issue in Washington and then in U.S. Embassies abroad. This also coincided with both Congressional and educational, and media interest in the subject. Newspapers, journals, books, and television reported on the subject. Although at first disparaged, *Dezinformatsia* —Disinformation, and *Aktivniye meropriyatiya*—Active Measures, and *Kombinatzia* — employing both overt and

---

[5] Office of the Director of National Intelligence, "Assessing Russian Activities and Intentions in Recent U.S. Elections," ICA 2017-01D, 6 January 2017.

[6] There is however, a dearth of public information of this subject.

[7] Fletcher Schoen and Christopher J. Lamb, *Deception, Disinformation, and Strategic Communications: How One Interagency Group Made A Major Difference*, Center for Strategic Research, Institute for National Strategic Studies, National Defense University, 2012.

covert techniques—entered into the lexicon in policy and academic circles, [8] much as *Kompromat* or compromising material has today.

The second result of the Soviet active measures in this period was to help stimulate the Administration and the Congress to actively promote abroad positive liberal principles and institutions, particularly electoral democracy, the rule of law, and human rights. Active involvement by the U.S. in the positive promotion of liberal principles had waxed and waned throughout the 20th Century. It now blossomed again. The U.S. did this unilaterally as well as in partnership with Allies and global and regional organizations. In part this was because the principles were considered part of the American heritage. But it was also because the U.S. had security interests in supporting democratic forces abroad who were competing with communism and Soviet influence, as well as with other illiberal actors such as organized crime and kleptocracy.

An outstanding example was the creation and continuation of bipartisan support and funding of what became the National Endowment for Democracy in 1984. It was focused on helping to support electoral democratic principles abroad. There were many other "whole of government" efforts to entertain smaller but sometimes effective projects, on religious freedom and toleration, and human rights.

It is difficult to assess the overall effectiveness of these efforts. There has been some evaluation of the U.S. performance. Some well-informed practitioners maintain that they were a major cause of the demise of the USSR – that it stimulated the final collapse of the Soviet system in Russia and Central and Eastern Europe.[9] Academics in particular tend to believe that there were multiple long and short-term causes of how and why the Soviet Union disintegrated.

But it happened, and as Americans have been wont to do after other successes abroad, interest in the competition between liberal and illiberal actors in world politics waned – as it had after World War I and World War II. After a few years at the turn of the 20th Century, illiberal actors in Russia regained control of the country with much of its active measures apparatus intact. In the main, we were again surprised.

---

[8] Richard Shultz and Roy Godson, *Dezinformatsia: Active Measures in Soviet Strategy.*.
[9] See for example, Kraemer, Sven F, Inside the Cold War from Marx to Reagan: An Unprecedented Guide to the Roots, History, Strategies, and Key Documents of the Cold War, UPA, 2015.

As far as we can see, the Putin regime, while not claiming a universal ideological solution to the world's problems as its predecessors did, nonetheless is working assiduously to gain and wield power and influence world-wide. The rise in oil prices, foreign investment, and advances in technology all fueled these efforts. More recently their economic and social position has weakened. But their continued propensity to use active measures so far has not diminished. Rather, it allows them once again to punch above their weight on the world scene and help shift the correlation of forces further in their favor without escalation to major war. They can do so because they never abandoned their playbook and many of their players.

What is to be Done

So what is to be done by the U.S. in the short and longer-term?

I hope that this Open Hearing in the Committee will contribute to a much enhanced U.S. diagnostic and prescriptive policy effort that will further cauterize an ongoing problem and perhaps avoid its escalation in the future. While we seek to understand the specifics and implications of contemporary Russian behavior we can also begin to peer over the horizon. The attentive U.S. public and elected officials really ought not to be surprised again – strategically or tactically.

To help understand future Russian thinking and capabilities the following initiatives are offered that may assist in doing so.

1. Identifying in Real Time and Anticipating Russian Active Measures.

2. Reducing Russian Effectiveness.

3. Developing a strategic approach to countering Russian Active Measures.

1. Identifying and anticipating Russian Active Measures

We need enhanced warning of real-time Russian planning and their development of active measures capabilities. The U.S. National Counterintelligence Strategy of 2016 does call for the collection and analysis of the threats from foreign intelligence. We also need to anticipate—not predict—Russia's likely future operations. This will not always be possible but we should at least try. These "warnings," in whole or in part, would be disseminated inside the U.S.

government, to selected allies, and some in the media and public so that there would be little surprise. The USG does this now with counterterrorism warnings.

2. Reducing Russian effectiveness.

We should develop and implement techniques to reduce the damage caused by the Russian active measures apparatus. To some extent this can be done by the careful dissemination and follow up of the warnings. But there are a variety of additional techniques we can use regularly that would appear to mitigate or reduce the damage. One is exposure of Russian plans and operations before or after the Active Measures play out in the U.S. and abroad. Again, this was done in the 1980s, under the auspices of the State Department and the interagency group.

Another is to disseminate a positive narrative to refute specific Russian attempts to undermine the democratic narrative. This has worked previously through the "whole of government" approach, but it needs to be reinstituted and enhanced.

3. Developing a strategic approach to countering Russian Active Measures. This is a policy as well as an intelligence issue. What should the U.S. expect and tolerate from Russia. Are there 'red lines' that should not be crossed? For example, should we tolerate Russian (and other) efforts to influence the mechanisms of our election process and its outcomes, now or in the future. As the FBI Director maintained recently,[10] we can expect them to be back—not necessarily using the same tactics – although past history suggests they tend to reuse successful ones.

How do we counter their techniques without escalating our national security problems? As one former practitioner-scholar put it, we have been able to learn how to do this with regard to nuclear weapons. There are "rules of the road" that both sides follow to avoid the catastrophe neither wants. Is there thought and research that needs to be devoted to active measures and new technologies, in addition to the Internet, that are already on the world stage with more to come?

---

[10] Comey, James B., Testimony Before the House Permanent Select Committee on Intelligence (HPSCI), Hearing, *Russian Active Measures Investigation*, March 20, 2017.

Should we confine ourselves to defensive, punitive methods such as sanctions? How do we respond to techniques such as "doxing" or stealing personal or government information and disclosing it at strategic moments such as elections or crises?

And should we be more politically assertive, for example, stepping up our support to elements of emerging liberal societies who are asking for our help to compete effectively against illiberal adversaries—through genuine education and advisory methods? [11]

***

Again, thank you for initiating this opportunity to address an issue of such great public concern today and for the foreseeable future.

---

[11] Phillips, *Rufus*, *"Breathing Life into* Expeditionary Diplomacy: *A Missing Dimension of U.S. Security Capabilities,"* National Strategy Information Center, 2014.

ACTIVE MEASURES

"Active Measures is a term that came into use in the 1950s to describe certain overt and covert techniques for influencing events and behavior in, and the action of, foreign countries. Active measures may entail influencing the policies of another government, undermining confidence in its leaders and institutions, disrupting relations between other nations, and discrediting and weakening governmental and non-governmental opponents. This frequently involves attempts to deceive the target (foreign governmental and non-governmental elites or mass audiences), and to distort the target's perception of reality.

Active Measures may be conducted overtly through officially-sponsored foreign propaganda channels, diplomatic relations, and cultural diplomacy. Covert political techniques include the use of covert propaganda, oral and written disinformation, agents of influence, clandestine radios, and international front organizations. Although active measures are principally political in nature, military maneuvers and paramilitary assistance to insurgent and terrorists may also be involved."

Extracted from Richard Shultz and Roy Godson, *Dezinformatsia: Active Measures in Soviet Strategy,* Pergamon-Brassey's, 1984.

Chairman BURR. Thank you, Dr. Godson.

Dr. Rumer.

STATEMENT OF EUGENE B. RUMER, Ph.D., SENIOR FELLOW AND DIRECTOR, RUSSIA AND EURASIA PROGRAM, CARNEGIE ENDOWMENT FOR INTERNATIONAL PEACE

Dr. RUMER. Chairman Burr, Vice Chairman Warner, distinguished members of the committee: I'm honored to be here today.

Russian active measures and interference in our presidential campaign is one of the most contentious issues in our national conversation. I believe that Russian intelligence services and their proxies intervened in our election in 2016. I have not seen the classified evidence behind the intelligence community assessment published a few weeks ago. Some have criticized it for not sharing the evidence of Russian intrusions. They miss the mark. It is the totality of Russian efforts in plain sight to mislead, to misinform, to exaggerate, that is more convincing than any cyber evidence. RT, Russia Today Broadcast, internet trolls, fake news, and so on are an integral part of Russian foreign policy to date.

We need to put this in the context of the quarter century since the end of the Cold War. World War II in Europe, or "the Great Patriotic War," as Russians call it, is integral to the formative experience of every living Russian. The country's national narrative is impossible without it.

In 1941 Hitler's armies were just outside the gates of Moscow. In 1945 Stalin's armies entered Berlin. That was Russia's greatest generation. Generations of Russians since then have been taught that their country was at its most secure then because it was protected by a buffer: the Warsaw Pact and the Soviet empire.

In 1991, Russians lost that buffer, the legacy of their greatest generation. With their country falling apart, Russian leaders had no choice but to accept this loss for as long as Russia would remain weak. The 1990s were a terrible decade for Russia, but a great decade for the West. For Russian leaders and many regular Russians, the dominance of the West came at the expense of Russia's loss in the Cold War.

But Russia would not remain weak indefinitely. Its economic recovery led to a return to a much more assertive posture, aggressive posture some would say, on the world stage. We saw it in the crushing of Georgia in 2008, in the annexation of Crimea in 2014, and we see it to the present day in the ongoing war in eastern Ukraine.

For the West, Russia's return to the world stage has been nothing more than pure revanchism. For Russia, it is restoring some balance in their relationship with the West. The narrative of restoring the balance, correcting the injustice and the distortions of the 1990s, has been the essential—has been absolutely essential to Russian propaganda since the beginning of the Putin era. Those Russians who disagree are branded as foreign agents and enemies of the people.

But Russia's capabilities should not be overestimated. Its GDP is about $1.3 trillion versus U.S. GDP of over $18 trillion. Russian defense spending is estimated at about $65 billion. That's little more than President Trump's proposed increase in U.S. defense spending for fiscal year 2018.

The Russian military is undeniably stronger than its smaller and weaker neighbors. Yet the balance does not favor Russia when compared to NATO. A NATO–Russia war would be an act of mutual suicide and the Kremlin is not ready for it.

Russian leaders have embraced a difficult toolkit—information warfare, intimidation, espionage, economic tools, and so on. This toolkit is meant to make up for Russia's conventional shortcomings vis-à-vis the West.

The Kremlin has a number of advantages here. The circle of deciders is limited to a handful of Putin associates with similar world views. They have considerable resources at their disposal, especially since most of their tools are quite cheap. A handful of cyber criminals costs a lot less than an armored brigade, but can do a lot of damage.

Russian meddling in our presidential election most likely is viewed by the Kremlin as an unqualified success. The payoffs include, but are not limited to: one, a major distraction to the United States, for the United States; damage to U.S. leadership in the world; and perhaps most importantly, the demonstration effect. The Kremlin can do this to the world's sole remaining global superpower. Imagine how other countries feel.

The differences between Russia and the United States are profound and will not be resolved soon. This is not a crisis, not something that will pass soon. It is the new normal. We will see Russia relying on this toolkit in the months and years to come, in the upcoming elections in France and in Germany this year, in our own future political campaigns.

Deception and active measures have long been and will remain a staple of Russian dealings with the outside world for the foreseeable future.

Thank you.

[The prepared statement of Dr. Rumer follows:]

CARNEGIE
ENDOWMENT FOR
INTERNATIONAL PEACE

RUSSIAN ACTIVE MEASURES AND INFLUENCE CAMPAIGNS

Eugene B. Rumer
Senior Fellow and Director
Russia and Eurasia Program
Carnegie Endowment for International Peace

Testimony before U.S. Senate Select Committee on Intelligence

March 30, 2017

Chairman Burr, Vice Chairman Warner, distinguished members of Senate Select Committee on Intelligence!

It is a great honor to appear here today. The issue before this panel is Russian active measures and influence campaigns. It rose to the top of our national agenda in 2016, when we became aware of Russian interference in our presidential campaign. It remains one of the most contentious issues in our national conversation, for the very idea that another nation could put at risk the integrity of our country's most essential institution—the process of electing our president—is hard for us to comprehend.

I would like to state at the outset that based on media reporting, on statements of senior U.S. and other countries' law enforcement and intelligence officials, and my professional experience as a student of Russian foreign policy, I am convinced that Russian intelligence services, their proxies, and other related actors directly intervened in our election in 2016.

You might ask why I am so confident of this. I have not seen the classified evidence that supports the findings presented in the Intelligence Community Assessment "Assessing Russian Activities and Intentions in Recent US Elections" published by the Office of the Director of National Intelligence on January 6, 2017. Some observers have been critical of that Assessment for not presenting detailed evidence of Russian cyber intrusions or covert activities. They miss the mark—it is the totality of the Russian effort to interfere, mislead, misinform, outright falsify, influence, etc. that is just as, if not more convincing than the cyber evidence of the Russian break in into the Democratic National Committee (DNC) server and other intrusions. That Russian effort is before us in plain sight—in state-sponsored propaganda broadcasts on RT (Russia Today), in countless internet trolls, fake or distorted news spread by fake news services, in the recent Kremlin get together of Russian president Vladimir Putin with the French far right presidential candidate Marine Le Pen. The list can go on. That effort is also an integral part of Russian foreign policy and domestic politics.

It's More than the Economy

To understand why the Russian government is engaged in this large-scale and diversified influence operation, which blends overt and covert activities, one needs to step back and put it in the context of events of the quarter century since the end of the Cold War.

Every country's foreign policy is a product of its history, its geography, and its politics. Russia is no exception to this rule, and to understand the pattern of Russian behavior at home and abroad, we need to look at Russian history, Russian geography, and Russian domestic politics.

War in Europe is integral to the formative experience of every Russian. The country's national narrative is impossible without the record of two wars—the Patriotic War of 1812, which Russians view as a war of liberation from Napoleon's invasion of Russia, and the Great Patriotic War of 1941-1945. Both wars were fought to liberate Patria, the Fatherland, from foreign occupiers. In 1812, Napoleon entered Moscow and the city was burned. In 1941, Hitler's armies were stopped just outside the city limits of Moscow. Americans, too, had their war of 1812, and Washington too was burned, but few Russians know or remember it, just as they think little of the fighting in the Pacific theater against Japan in the second world war. Stalin's armies didn't enter it until nearly the very end, three months after the war in Europe ended. The end of the Great Patriotic War is celebrated in Russia every year as a great national holiday on May 9. The greatest Russian novel of all times is Leo Tolstoy's *War and Peace*, all Russians read it in high school. They are also taught in history classes that their country's greatest accomplishment of the 20th century was the defeat of fascism in the Great Patriotic War.

The war of 1812 ended for Russia when the armies of Tsar Alexander I entered Paris in 1814. The Great Patriotic War ended in 1945 when Stalin's armies entered Berlin. From 1945 to 1989, when the Berlin Wall came down, Russia was at its most secure, or so successive generations of Russian leaders have been taught to believe. The history and the strategy taught in Russian military academies for decades after it ended were the history and the strategy of the Great Patriotic War. The map for tabletop exercises at the Military Academy of the General Staff in 2001 was a giant map of the European theater. U.S. strategists were by that time "done" with Europe and shifting their focus from the Balkan edge of the continent to South Asia and the Middle East. Russia was not "done" with Europe.

Little appreciated in the West at the time was the trauma suffered by the Russian national security establishment when it lost its outer and inner security buffers—the Warsaw Pact and the Soviet empire. The sense of physical security afforded by this dual buffer between NATO's armies and the Russian heartland was gone. Russian declaratory policy may have been to sign on to the 1990 Charter of Paris as the Cold War ended, but the historical legacy and the geography of Russian national security could not be altered with the stroke of a pen. Even as the Communist system was dismantled and the Soviet Union disbanded, Russia's national security establishment, which had been brought up for generations to think in terms of hard power, could not and did not embrace the new vision of European security based on shared values.

In 1991, with their society in turmoil, their economy in tatters, their military in retreat from the outer and inner empires, and their country literally falling apart, Russian leaders had no choice but to go along with that vision. They also accepted as given that history is written by the victors, and that the victors would also make the rules for the new era. Russia would have to go along with it for as long as it remained weak.

The 1990s were a terrible decade for Russia. Its domestic politics remained in turmoil, its economy limped from one crisis to the next, and its international standing—only recently that of a superpower—collapsed. Western students of Russia were entertaining the prospect of a world without Russia. It was not lost on Russian political elites that the 1990s were also a time of great prosperity and global influence for the West. For them, brought up on the idea of importance of hard power, the dominance of the West was inextricably tied to its victory in the Cold War, the defeat of Russia, its retreat from the world stage, and the expansion of the West in its wake.

Russia Is Back

But Russia would not remain weak indefinitely. Its economic recovery after the turn of the century, buoyed by soaring global prices for commodities and hydrocarbons, and its domestic political consolidation around Vladimir Putin and his brand of increasingly authoritarian leadership, so different from the leadership of Boris Yeltsin, have laid the groundwork for a return to Russia's more assertive posture on the world stage.

That increasingly assertive posture has manifested itself on multiple occasions and in different forms over the past decade and a half—in Vladimir Putin's speech at the Munich Security Conference in 2007; in the war with Georgia in 2008 and the statement in its aftermath by then-president Dmitry Medvedev about Russia's claim to a sphere of "privileged interests" around its periphery; and finally in the annexation of Crimea in 2014 and the undeclared war in eastern Ukraine to keep Ukraine from slipping from Russia's orbit.

For the West, Russia's return to the world stage has been nothing more than pure revanchism. It violates the basic, core principles of the post-Cold War European security architecture—which Russia pledged to observe over a quarter-century ago.

For Russia, it is restoring a balance—not the old balance, but some semblance of it. Currently, NATO troops are deployed to deter Russian aggression against Estonia. (Curiously, former speaker of the House Newt Gingrich has described it as the "suburbs of St. Petersburg.") Russia's security establishment views this commitment by NATO countries to its vulnerable ally as a threat to the heartland.

The narrative of restoring the balance, correcting the injustice and the distortions of the 1990s, when the West took advantage of Russia's weakness, has been the essential element of Russian state-sponsored propaganda since the beginning of the Putin era. Whether or not we choose to accept this narrative, these beliefs undergird Russia's comeback on the world stage and political consolidation at home. In public and private, top Russian officials proclaim that the wars in Georgia and Ukraine were fought to prevent Western encroachment on territories vital to Russian security. The military deployment in Syria merely restores Russia's traditional foothold in the Middle East, from which Russia withdrew when it was weak, and where it was replaced by the West with consequences that have been tragic for the entire region.

In domestic politics, Putin's authoritarian restoration is treated by the majority of average and elite members of Russian society as the return to the country's traditional political health, free from foreign interference in its political and economic life. The more pluralistic system and dramatic decline of the 1990s are linked in this narrative to the influence of the United States and other foreign interests in Russia's economy and politics, to their desire to introduce alien values in Russia's political culture and take Russia's oil. U.S. support for Russian civil society is an effort to undermine the Russian state, to bring Russia back to its knees, and take advantage of it, both at home and abroad. Western economic sanctions imposed on Russia in the wake of its annexation of Crimea and the undeclared war in eastern Ukraine are a form of warfare designed to weaken

Russia and gain unfair advantage over it. Western support for democracy in countries around Russia's periphery is an effort to encircle it and weaken it too.

This narrative has dominated the airwaves inside Russia, where the Kremlin controls the television, which is the principal medium that delivers news to most Russians. With independent media in retreat and alternative sources of information marginalized, this narrative has struck a responsive chord with many Russians. The narrative has been effective because it contains an element of truth—Russia did implode in the 1990s, and the West prospered; Russia did recover from its troubles and regained a measure of its global standing on Putin's watch; the West did promote democracy in Russia, which coincided with its time of troubles; and the West has been critical of the Russian government's retreat from democracy as Russia regained strength.

Moreover, foreign policy traditionally was and is the preserve of the country's political elite and its small national security establishment. Whereas there are some voices inside Russia who, like the leading anti-corruption activist Alexei Navalny, have challenged the many domestic failings and authoritarian leanings of the Putin government, there are hardly any who have challenged its foreign policy record. Worse yet, the Kremlin propaganda has been apparently so effective, and the legal constraints imposed by it so severe, that few Russian opposition voices dare to challenge the government's foreign policy course for fear of being branded as foreign agents, enemies of the people, and fifth columnists.

Warfare by Other Means

For all the talk about Russian recovery and resurgence on the world stage, its capabilities should not be overestimated. Its GDP is about $1.3 trillion vs. U.S. GDP of over $18 trillion. The Russian economy is not "in shambles," but in the words of a leading Russian government economist it is doomed to "eternal stagnation" unless the government undertakes major new reforms.

Russian defense expenditures are estimated at about $65 billion, or little more than President Trump's proposed increase in U.S. defense spending for FY 2018. The Russian military is estimated at just over 750,000—well short of its authorized strength of one million—vs. U.S. 1.4 million active duty military personnel.

By all accounts, the Russian military has made huge strides in the past decade, benefiting from far-reaching reforms and generous defense spending. It is undeniably far superior militarily to its smaller, weaker neighbors and enjoys considerable geographic advantages in theaters around its periphery.

Yet, the overall military balance does not favor Russia when it is compared to the United States and its NATO allies. They have bigger economies, spend more on defense, have bigger, better equipped militaries, and are more technologically sophisticated. A NATO-Russia war would be an act of mutual suicide, and the Kremlin is not ready for it. Its campaign against the West has to be prosecuted by other means.

That is the backdrop for the subject of today's hearings. Since Russia cannot compete toe-to-toe with the West, its leaders have embraced a wide range of tools—information warfare in all its forms, including subversion, deception, dis- and mis-information, intimidation, espionage, economic tools, including sanctions, bribery, selective favorable trading regimes, influence campaigns, etc. This toolkit has deep historical roots in the Soviet era and performs the function of the equalizer that in the eyes of the Kremlin is intended to make up for Russia's weakness vis-à-vis the West.

In employing this toolkit, the Kremlin has a number of important advantages. There is no domestic audience before which it has to account for its actions abroad. The Kremlin has few, if any external restraints in employing it, and its decisionmaking mechanism is streamlined. There is no legislature to report to, for the Duma is a rubber stamp body eager to sign off on any Kremlin foreign policy initiative.

The circle of deciders is far smaller than the Soviet-era Politburo, and it is limited to a handful of Putin associates with similar worldviews and backgrounds. They are determined to carry on an adversarial relationship with the West. They can make decisions quickly and have considerable resources at their disposal, especially given the relatively inexpensive nature of most of the tools they rely on. A handful of cyber criminals cost a lot less than an armored brigade and can cause a great deal more damage with much smaller risks.

Shame and reputational risks do not appear to be a factor in Russian decision-making. In early-2016, Russian Foreign Minister Sergei Lavrov did not shy away from repeating a patently false fake media story about the rape of a Russian-German girl by a Syrian asylum-seeker in Germany.

Moreover, a version of selective naming and shaming—or targeting of political adversaries with false allegations of misconduct—has been used by Russian propaganda to discredit political adversaries in the West. Russian propaganda, and Putin personally, have sought to deflect the attention from the fact of the intrusion into the DNC server and the top leadership of Hillary Clinton's presidential campaign to the information released as a result of it that has presented various political operatives in an unfavorable light.

This not only deflects the attention from Russia's role in this episode, it helps the Kremlin convey an important message to its domestic audience about the corrupt nature of U.S. politics. Russia therefore is no worse than the United States, which has no right to complain about corruption and democracy deficit in Russia.

Russian meddling in the 2016 U.S. presidential election is likely to be seen by the Kremlin as a major success regardless of whether its initial goal was to help advance the Trump candidacy. The payoff includes, but is not limited to a major political disruption in the United States, which has been distracted from many strategic pursuits; the standing of the United States and its leadership in the world have been damaged; it has become a common theme in the narrative of many leading commentators that from the pillar of stability of the international liberal order the United States has been transformed into its biggest source of instability; U.S. commitments to key allies in Europe and Asia have been questioned on both sides of the Atlantic and the Pacific. And last, but not least, the Kremlin has demonstrated what it can do to the world's sole remaining global superpower.

It Is Not a Crisis, It Is the New Normal

Events of the past three years, since the annexation of Crimea by Russia, have been referred to as a crisis in relations between Russia and the West. However, this is no longer a crisis. The differences between Russia and the West are profound and are highly unlikely to be resolved in the foreseeable future without one or the other side capitulating. The U.S.-Russian relationship is fundamentally broken, and this situation should be treated as the new normal rather than an exceptional period in our relations. For the foreseeable future our relationship is likely to remain competitive and, at times, adversarial.

The full extent of Russian meddling in the 2016 presidential election is not yet publicly known. But the melding of various tools (e.g, the use of cyber operations to collect certain information covertly) and the provision of this information to outlets such as Wikileaks and the news media was certainly a first. Unfortunately, it is not a first for U.S. allies and partners in Europe and Eurasia. It is not the last either. Just a few days ago, Vladimir Putin received France's right-wing presidential candidate Marine Le Pen in the Kremlin. Previously, her National Front had received a loan from a Moscow-based bank, and Russian media outlets have tried to injure the reputation of her chief opponent Emmanuel Macron by spreading rumors about his sexuality and ties to financial institutions. The chiefs of British and German intelligence services have warned publicly about the threat from Russia to their countries' democratic processes. The Netherlands recently chose to forego reliance on certain computer vote tabulation systems due to elevated fears of Russian interference and hacking.

The experience of Russian meddling in the 2016 U.S. election should be judged an unqualified success for the Kremlin. It has cost it little and paid off in more ways than can be easily counted. To be sure, U.S. officials should expect it to be repeated again and again in the future. 2016 was a crisis, but it was not an aberration and should be treated as the new normal. Cyber is merely a new domain. Deception and active measures in all their incarnations have long been and will remain a staple of Russia's dealings with the outside world for the foreseeable future.

Chairman BURR. Dr. Rumer, thank you.
Mr. Watts.

STATEMENT OF CLINT WATTS, ROBERT A. FOX FELLOW, FOREIGN POLICY RESEARCH INSTITUTE

Mr. WATTS. Mr. Chairman, members of the committee: thank you for inviting me here today.

In April 2014, Andrew Weisburd, J.M. Berger, and I noticed a petition on the WhiteHouse.gov website. "Alaska Back to Russia" appeared as a public campaign to give America's largest state back to the nation from which it was purchased. Satirical or nonsensical petitions appearing on the White House website are not out of the norm. But this petition was different, having gained more than 39,000 online signatures in a short period.

Our examining of those signing and posting on this petition revealed an odd pattern. The accounts varied considerably from other petitions and appeared to be the work of bots. A closer look at those bots tied in closely with other social media campaigns we had observed pushing Russian propaganda months before. Hackers proliferated the networks and could be spotted among recent data breaches and website defacements. Closely circling those hackers were honeypot accounts, attractive-looking women and political partisans that were trying to social engineer other users.

Above all, we observed hecklers, those synchronized trolling accounts you see on Twitter that would attack political targets using similar talking patterns and points. Those accounts, some of which overtly support the Kremlin, promoted Russian foreign policy positions targeting key English-speaking audiences throughout Europe and North America.

Soviet active measures strategy and tactics have been reborn and updated for the modern Russian regime and the digital age. Today Russia hopes to win the second Cold War through the force of politics, as opposed to the politics of force.

While Russia certainly seeks to promote Western candidates sympathetic to their worldview and foreign policy objectives, winning a single election is not their end goal. Russian active measures hope to topple democracies through the pursuit of five complementary objectives:

One, undermine citizen confidence in democratic governance;

Two, foment and exacerbate divisive political fissures;

Three, erode trust between citizens and elected officials and their institutions;

Four, popularize Russian policy agendas within foreign populations;

And five, create general distrust or confusion over information sources by blurring the lines between fact and fiction, a very pertinent issue today in our country.

From these objectives, the Kremlin can crumble democracies from the inside out, achieving two key milestones: one, the dissolution of the European Union; and two, the breakup of NATO. Achieving these two victories against the West will allow Russia to reassert its power globally and pursue its foreign policy objectives bilaterally through military, diplomatic, and economic aggression.

In late 2014 and throughout 2015, we watched active measures on nearly any disaffected U.S. audience. Whether it be claims of the U.S. military declaring martial law during the Jade Helm exercise, chaos amongst Black Lives Matter protests, or a standoff at the Bundy Ranch, Russia's state-sponsored RT and Sputnik News, characterized as white outlets, churned out manipulated truths, false news stories, and conspiracies. They generally lined up under four themes:

One, political messages designed to tarnish democratic leaders and institutions;

Two, financial propaganda, created to weaken confidence in financial markets and capitalist economies;

Three, social unrest, crafted to amplify divisions amongst democratic populaces;

And four, global calamity, pushed to incite fear of global demise, such as nuclear war or catastrophic climate change.

From these overt Russian propaganda outlets, a wide range of English-speaking conspiratorial websites, which we refer to as gray outlets, some of which mysteriously operate from Eastern Europe and are curiously led by pro-Russian editors of unknown financing, sensationalize these conspiracies and fake news published by white outlets.

American-looking social media accounts, hecklers, honeypots, and hackers I described earlier, working alongside automated bots, further amplify this Russian propaganda amongst unwitting Westerners.

Through the end of 2015, the start of 2016, the Russian influence system began pushing themes and messages seeking to influence the outcome of the U.S. presidential election. Russia's overt media outlets and covert trolls sought to sideline opponents on both sides of the political spectrum with adversarial views toward the Kremlin. They were in full swing during both the Republican and Democratic primary season and may have helped sink the hopes of candidates more hostile to Russian interests long before the field narrowed. Senator Rubio, in my opinion you anecdotally suffered from these efforts.

The final piece of Russia's modern active measures surfaced in the summer of 2016 as hacked materials were strategically leaked. The disclosures of WikiLeaks, Guccifer 2.0, and DCLeaks demonstrated how hacks would power the influence system Russia had built so successfully in the previous two years.

As an example, on the evening of 30 July 2016 my colleagues and I watched as RT and Sputnik News simultaneously launched false stories of the U.S. air base at Incirlik, Turkey, being overrun by terrorists. Within minutes, pro-Russian social media aggregators and automated bots amplified this false news story. More than 4,000 tweets in the first 78 minutes after launching this false story going back to the active measures accounts we had tracked in the previous two years.

These previously identified accounts almost simultaneously, appearing from difficult geographic locations and communities, amplified the fake news story in unison. The hashtags pushed by these accounts were "nuclear," "media," "Trump," and "Benghazi." The most common words found in English-speaking Twitter profiles were "God," "military," "Trump," "family," "country," "conservative," "Christian," "America," and "Constitution."

These accounts and their messages clearly sought to convince Americans a U.S. military base was being overrun in a terrorist attack. In reality, a small protest gathered outside the gate and the increased security at the air base sought to secure the arrival of the Chairman of the Joint Chiefs.

Many of the accounts we watched push the false Incirlik story today focus on the elections in Europe, promoting fears of immigration or false claims of refugee criminality. They have not forgotten about the U.S., either. This past week we observed social media accounts discrediting Speaker of the House Paul Ryan, hoping to further foment unrest inside U.S. democratic institutions.

The implications of Russia's new active measures model will be twofold. The first is what the world is witnessing today, a Russian challenge to democracy throughout the West. But more importantly, over the horizon Russia has provided any authoritarian dictator or predatory elite equipped with hackers and disrespectful of civil liberties a playbook to dismantle their enemies through information warfare.

The U.S., in failing to respond to active measures, will surrender its position as the world's leader, forego its role as chief promoter and defender of democracy, and give up on over 70 years of collective action to preserve freedom and civil liberties around the world.

Russia's strategic motto for America and the West is: "Divided they stand and divided they will fall." It's time the United States reminds the world that, despite our day to day policy debates and political squabbles, we stand united alongside our allies in defending our democratic system of government from the meddling of power-hungry tyrants and repressive authoritarians that prey on their people and suppress humanity.

I'll close here with my opening remarks, but I have many recommendations which are in my written testimony. Mr. Chairman, I ask that my full written statement, which includes these recommendations, be submitted for the record, and I hope that during the question and answer session we can further discuss how we might counter these active measures. Thank you for inviting me.

[The prepared statement of Mr. Watts follows:]

Clint Watts
- **Robert A. Fox Fellow, Foreign Policy Research Institute**
- **Senior Fellow, Center for Cyber and Homeland Security, the George Washington University**

Statement Prepared for the U.S. Senate Select Committee on Intelligence hearing:

"Disinformation: A Primer In Russian Active Measures And Influence Campaigns"

30 March 2017

On 26 October 2015, I authored a post at the Foreign Policy Research Institute (FPRI) entitled "Russia Returns As Al Qaeda And The Islamic State's Far Enemy" noting:

> *"The Russians have used social media driven information campaigns to discredit the U.S. for years. Facebook and Twitter remain littered with pro-Russian, Western looking accounts and supporting automated bots designed to undermine the credibility of the U.S. government."*[1]

Just a few weeks later in November 2015, the FBI visited FPRI notifying their leadership that I had been targeted by a cyber attack. The FBI didn't say who exactly had targeted me, but I had a good idea who it might be.

In the eighteen months prior to the above quote and in the three years leading up to today, two colleagues and I watched and tracked the rise of Russia's social media influence operations witnessing their update of an old Soviet playbook known as Active Measures.

For me, I began watching these influence operations in January 2014 after I co-authored an article in *Foreign Affairs* entitled "The Good and The Bad of Ahrar al Sham."[2] Hecklers appearing to be English-speaking Europeans and Americans trolled me for my stance on Syrian President Bashar Assad. But these social media accounts, they didn't look right - their aggression, persistence, biographies, speech patterns and synchronization were unnatural. I wasn't the only one who noticed this pattern. Andrew Weisburd and J.M. Berger, the two best social media analysts I'd worked with in counterterrorism, noticed similar patterns around the troll discussions of Syria, Assad, al Qaeda and the Islamic State.

---

[1] Clint Watts (26 October 2015) *Russia returns as al Qaeda and the Islamic State's 'Far Enemy'*. Foreign Policy Research Institute. Available at:
http://www.fpri.org/2015/10/russia-returns-as-al-qaeda-and-the-islamic-states-far-enemy/
[2] Michael Doran, William McCants and Clint Watts (23 January 2014) *The Good and Bad of Ahrar al-Sham*. Foreign Affairs. Available at:
https://www.foreignaffairs.com/articles/syria/2014-01-23/good-and-bad-ahrar-al-sham

Shortly after, in March 2014, we noticed a petition on the WhiteHouse.gov website. "Alaska Back To Russia" appeared as a public campaign to give America's largest state back to the nation from which it was purchased.[3] Satirical or nonsensical petitions appearing on the White House website are not out of the norm. This petition was different though, having gained more than 39,000 online signatures in a short time period. Our examination of those signing and posting on this petition revealed an odd pattern -- the accounts varied considerably from other petitions and appeared to be the work of automated bots. These bots tied in closely with other social media campaigns we had observed pushing Russian propaganda.

Through the summer and fall of 2014, we studied these pro-Russia accounts and automated bots. Hackers proliferated the networks and could be spotted amongst recent data breaches and website defacements. Closely circling them were honeypot accounts, attractive looking women or passionate political partisans, which appeared to be befriending certain audience members through social engineering. Above all, we observed hecklers, synchronized trolling accounts that would attack political targets using similar talking points and follower patterns. These accounts, some of which overtly supported the Kremlin, promoted Russian foreign policy positions targeting key English speaking audiences throughout Europe and North America. From this pattern, we realized we were observing a deliberate, well organized, well resourced, well funded, wide ranging effort commanded by only one possible adversary – Russia.

Active Measures: Everything Old Is New Again

Soviet Active Measures strategy and tactics have been reborn and updated for the modern Russian regime and the digital age. Today, Russia seeks to win the second Cold War through "the force of politics as opposed to the politics of force".[4] As compared to the analog information wars of the first Cold War, the Internet and social media provide Russia cheap, efficient and highly effective access to foreign audiences with plausible deniability of their influence.

Russia's new and improved online Active Measures shifted aggressively toward U.S. audiences in late 2014 and throughout 2015. They launched divisive messages on nearly any disaffected U.S. audience. Whether it be claims of the U.S. military declaring martial law during the Jade Helm exercise[5], chaos amongst Black Lives matter protests[6]

---

[3] The original petition is no longer accessible on the White House website but a summary of the campaign can be found at: Soraya Sarhaddi Nelson (1 April 2014) *Not An April Fools' Joke: Russians Petition To Get Alaska Back.* NPR. Available at: https://www.foreignaffairs.com/articles/syria/2014-01-23/good-and-bad-ahrar-al-sham

[4] U.S. Information Agency (June 1992) *Soviet Active Measures in the "Post Cold War" Era 1988-1991.* U.S. House of Representatives Committee on Appropriations. Available at: http://intellit.muskingum.edu/russia_folder/pcw_era/exec_sum.htm

[5] Dan Lamothe (14 September 2015) *Remember Jade Helm 15, the controversial military exercise? It's over.* Washington Post. Available at:

or tensions in the Bundy Ranch standoff in Oregon[7], Russia's state sponsored outlets of RT and Sputnik News, characterized as "white" influence efforts in information warfare, churned out manipulated truths, false news stories and conspiracies. Four general themes outlined these propaganda messages:

- Political Messages – Designed to tarnish democratic leaders and undermine democratic institutions
- Financial Propaganda – Created to weaken confidence in financial markets, capitalist economies and Western companies
- Social Unrest – Crafted to amplify divisions amongst democratic populaces to undermine citizen trust and the fabric of society
- Global Calamity – Pushed to incite fear of global demise such as nuclear war or catastrophic climate change

From these overt Russian propaganda outlets, a wide range of English language conspiratorial websites ("gray" outlets), some of which mysteriously operate from Eastern Europe and are curiously led by pro-Russian editors of unknown financing, sensationalize conspiracies and fake news published by white outlets further amplifying their reach in American audiences. American looking social media accounts, the hecklers, honeypots and hackers described above, working alongside automated bots further amplify and disseminate Russian propaganda amongst unwitting Westerners. These covert, "black" operations influence target audience opinions with regards to Russia and undermine confidence in Western elected leaders, public officials, mainstream media personalities, academic experts and democracy itself.

Through the end of 2015 and start of 2016, the Russian influence system outlined above began pushing themes and messages seeking to influence the outcome of the U.S. Presidential election. Russia's overt media outlets and covert trolls sought to sideline opponents on both sides of the political spectrum with adversarial views toward the Kremlin. The final months leading up to the election have been the predominate focus of Russian influence discussions to date. However, Russian Active Measures were in full swing during both the Republican and Democratic primary season and may have helped sink the hopes of candidates more hostile to Russian interests long before the field narrowed.

The final piece of Russia's modern Active Measures surfaced in the summer of 2016 as hacked materials from previous months were strategically leaked. On 22 July 2016, Wikileaks released troves of stolen communications from the Democratic National

---

https://www.washingtonpost.com/news/checkpoint/wp/2015/09/14/remember-jade-helm-15-the-controversial-military-exercise-its-over/?utm_term=.10e43e79bbc8
[6] (2 October 2016) *Tensions at rival White & Black Lives Matter protests flare in Houston*. RT. Available at: https://www.rt.com/usa/361346-blm-wlm-protests-houston/
[7] (20 December 2016) *Hands up or charging? Conflicting reports on shooting of Oregon militia spokesman*. RT. Available at: https://www.rt.com/usa/330365-oregon-lavoy-shooting-police/

Committee and later batches of campaign emails. Guccifer 2.0 and DC Leaks revealed hacked information from a host of former U.S. government officials throughout July and August 2016. For the remainder of the campaign season, this compromising material powered the influence system Russia successfully constructed in the previous two years.

On the evening of 30 July 2016, my colleagues and I watched as RT and Sputnik News simultaneously launched false stories of the U.S. airbase at Incirlik being overrun by terrorists. Within minutes, pro-Russian social media aggregators and automated bots amplified this false news story and expanded conspiracies asserting American nuclear missiles at the base would be lost to extremists. More than 4,000 tweets in the first 78 minutes after launching of this false story linked back to the Active Measures accounts we'd tracked in the previous two years. These previously identified accounts, almost simultaneously appearing from different geographic locations and communities, amplified this fake news story in unison. The hashtags incrementally pushed by these automated accounts were #Nuclear, #Media, #Trump and #Benghazi. The most common words found in English speaking Twitter user profiles were: God, Military, Trump, Family, Country, Conservative, Christian, America, and Constitution. These accounts and their messages clearly sought to convince Americans a U.S. military base was being overrun in a terrorist attack like the 2012 assault on a U.S. installation in Benghazi, Libya.[8] In reality, a small protest gathered outside the Incirlik gate and the increased security at the airbase sought to secure the arrival of the U.S. Chairman of the Joint Chiefs of Staff the following day.[9]

This pattern of Russian falsehoods and social media manipulation of the American electorate continued through Election Day and persists today. Many of the accounts we watched push the false Incirlik story in July now focus their efforts on shaping the upcoming European elections, promoting fears of immigration or false claims of refugee criminality. They've not forgotten about the United States either. This past week, we observed social media campaigns targeting Speaker of the House Paul Ryan hoping to foment further unrest amongst U.S. democratic institutions, their leaders and their constituents.

As we noted two days before the Presidential election in our article describing Russian influence operations, Russia certainly seeks to promote Western candidates sympathetic to their worldview and foreign policy objectives. But winning a single election is not

---

[8] Andrew Weisburd and Clint Watts (6 August 2016) *How Russia Dominates Your Twitter Feed to Promote Lies.* The Daily Beast. Available at: http://www.thedailybeast.com/articles/2016/08/06/how-russia-dominates-your-twitter-feed-to-promote-lies-and-trump-too.html

[9] (1 August 2016) *Chairman in Turkey to Meet With U.S. Troops, Turkish Officials.* U.S. Department of Defense. Available at: https://www.defense.gov/News/Article/Article/881458/chairman-in-turkey-to-meet-with-us-troops-turkish-officials

their end goal.[10] Russian Active Measures hope to topple democracies through the pursuit of five complementary objectives:

- Undermine citizen confidence in democratic governance
- Foment and exacerbate divisive political fractures
- Erode trust between citizens and elected officials and democratic institutions
- Popularize Russian policy agendas within foreign populations
- Create general distrust or confusion over information sources by blurring the lines between fact and fiction

From these objectives, the Kremlin can crumble democracies from the inside out creating political divisions resulting in two key milestones: 1) the dissolution of the European Union and 2) the break up of the North American Treaty Organization (NATO). Achieving these two victories against the West will allow Russia to reassert its power globally and pursue its foreign policy objectives bilaterally through military, diplomatic and economic aggression. Russia's undeterred annexation of Crimea, conflict in Ukraine and military deployment in Syria provide recent examples.

Why did Soviet Active Measures fail during the Cold War but succeed for Russia today?

Russia's Active Measures today work far better than that of their Soviet forefathers. During the Cold War, the KGB had to infiltrate the West, recruit agents and promote communist parties and their propaganda while under watch by Western counterintelligence efforts. Should they be too aggressive, Soviet spies conducting Active Measures amongst U.S. domestic groups could potentially trigger armed conflict or would be detained and deported.

Social media provides Russia's new Active Measures access to U.S. audiences without setting foot in the country, and the Kremlin smartly uses these platforms in seven ways to win Western elections. First, Russia chooses close democratic contests where a slight nudge can usher in their preferred candidate or desired outcome. Second, Russia targets specific audiences inside electorates amenable to their messages and resulting influence – in particular alt-right audiences incensed over immigration, refugees and economic hardship. Third, Russia plans and implements their strategy long before an election allowing sufficient time for cultivating an amenable audience ripe for manipulation. Fourth, their early entry into electoral debates allows them to test many messages and then reinforce those messages that resonate and bring about a measurable, preferred shift in public opinion. Fifth, Russia brilliantly uses hacking to compromise adversaries and power their influence messaging – a tactic most countries would not take. Sixth, their employment of social media automation saturates their intended audience with narratives

---

[10] Andrew Weisburd, Clint Watts and JM Berger (6 November 2016) *Trolling For Trump: How Russia Is Trying To Destroy Our Democracy.* War On The Rocks. Available at: https://warontherocks.com/2016/11/trolling-for-trump-how-russia-is-trying-to-destroy-our-democracy/

that drown out opposing viewpoints. Finally, Russia plays either side should the contest change – backing an individual candidate or party so long as they support a Kremlin policy position and then turning against the same party should their position shift against Russia.[11]

The implications of Russia's new Active Measures model will be two fold. The first is what the world is witnessing today – a Russian challenge to democracies throughout the West. Russian influence surfaced in Eastern Europe elections and the United Kingdom's Brexit vote before the U.S. Presidential election, helped bolster a losing far-right candidate recently in the Netherlands[12] and right now works diligently to shape the upcoming 2017 elections in France and Germany. Over the horizon, Russia has provided any authoritarian dictator or predatory elite equipped with hackers and disrespectful of civil liberties a playbook to dismantle their enemies through information warfare. Fledgling democracies and countries rife with ethnic and social divisions will be particularly vulnerable to larger authoritarian regimes with the time, resources and patience to foment chaos in smaller republics.

The U.S. Can Counter Russia's Modern Active Measures

America can defuse Russia's Active Measures online by undertaking a coordinated and broad range of actions across the U.S. government. Currently, the U.S. ignores, to its own detriment, falsehoods and manipulated truths generated and promoted by Russia's state sponsored media and their associated conspiratorial websites. While many Active Measures claims seem ridiculous, a non-response by the U.S. government introduces doubt and fuels social media conspiracies. The U.S. should generate immediate public refutations to false Russian claims by creating two official government webpages acting as a U.S. government "Snopes" for disarming falsehoods. The U.S. State Department would host a website responding to false claims regarding U.S. policy and operations outside U.S. borders. The U.S. Department of Homeland Security would host a parallel website responding to any and all false claims regarding U.S. policy and operations domestically – a particularly important function in times of emergency where Russian Active Measures have been observed inciting panic.

Criminal investigations bringing hackers to justice will continue to be vital. However, the FBI must take a more proactive role during investigations to analyze what information has been stolen by Russia and then help officials publicly disclose the breach in short order. Anticipating rather than reacting to emerging Russian data dumps through public

---

[11] Clint Watts and Andrew Weisburd (13 December 2016) *How Russia Wins An Election.* Politico. Available at: http://www.politico.com/magazine/story/2016/12/how-russia-wins-an-election-214524

[12] Andrew Higgins (27 February 2017) *Fake News, Fake Ukrainians: How a Group of Russians Tilted a Dutch Vote.* New York Times. Available at: https://www.nytimes.com/2017/02/16/world/europe/russia-ukraine-fake-news-dutch-vote.html

affairs messaging will help U.S. officials and other American targets of kompromat prepare themselves for future discrediting campaigns.

Russian propaganda sometime peddles false financial stories causing rapid shifts in American company stock prices that hurt consumer and investor confidence and open the way for predatory market manipulation and short selling. At times, U.S. business employees unwittingly engage with Russian social media hecklers and honeypots putting themselves and their companies at risk. The Departments of Treasury and Commerce should immediately undertake an education campaign for U.S. businesses to help them thwart damaging, false claims and train their employees in spotting nefarious social media operations that might compromise their information.

The Department of Homeland Security must continue to improve existing public-private partnerships and expand sharing of cyber trends and technical signatures. This information will be critical in helping citizens and companies prevent the hacking techniques propelling Russian kompromat. Finally, U.S. intelligence agencies have a large role to play in countering Russian Active Measures in the future, but my recommendations in this regard are not well suited for open discussion.

The most important actions to diffuse Russia's modern Active Measures actually come from outside the U.S. government – the private sector and civil society. Russia's social media influence campaigns achieve great success because mainstream media outlets amplify the salacious claims coming from stolen information. If forewarned by law enforcement of a Russian compromise (as noted above), the world's largest newspapers, cable news channels and social media companies could join in a pact vowing not to report on stolen information that amplified Russia's influence campaigns. While they would stand to lose audience in the near term to fringe outlets, Russia's Active Measures would be far less effective at discrediting their adversaries and shaping polities if they lacked access to mainstream media outlets. Mainstream media outlets unifying and choosing not to be Kremlin pawns would also be a counter to Russia's suppression of free speech and harsh treatment of journalists and the press.

Social media companies have played an outsized role in recent elections as they increasingly act as the primary news provider for their users. Tailored news feeds from social media platforms have created information bubbles where voters see only stories and opinions suiting their preferences and biases – ripe conditions for Russian disinformation campaigns.[13] In the lead up to the 2016 election, fake news stories were consumed at higher rates than true stories.[14] As a result, Facebook initiated a noble effort

---

[13] Yochai Benkler, Robert Faris, Hal Roberts and Ethan Zuckerman (3 March 2017) Study: Breitbart right-wing media ecosystem altered broader media agenda. Columbia Journalism Review. Available at: http://www.cjr.org/analysis/breitbart-media-trump-harvard-study.php

[14] Craig Silverman (18 November 2016) *This Analysis Shows How Viral Fake Election Stories Outperformed Real News On Facebook*. Buzzfeed. Available at:

to tag fake news stories for their readers.[15] But Facebook's push must be expanded and joined by other social media companies or they will be overwhelmed by the volume of stories needing evaluation and will find difficulty protecting freedom of speech and the freedom of the press.

Social media companies should band together in the creation of an Information Consumer Reports. This non-governmental agency would evaluate all media organizations, mainstream and otherwise, across a range of variables producing news ratings representative of the outlet's accuracy and orientation. The score would appear next to each outlet's content in web searches and social media streams providing the equivalent of a nutrition label for information. Consumers would not be restricted from viewing fake news outlets and their erroneous information, but would know the risks of their consumption. The rating, over time, would reduce consumption of Russian disinformation specifically and misinformation collectively, while also placing a check on mainstream media outlets that have all too often regurgitated false stories.[16]

Over the past three years, Russia has implemented and run the most effective and efficient influence campaign in world history.[17] Russian propaganda and social media manipulation has not stopped since the election in November and continues fomenting chaos amongst the American populace. American allies in Europe today suffer from an onslaught of hacks and manipulation, which threaten alliances that brought U.S. victory in the Cold War. The U.S., in failing to respond to Russia's Active Measures, will surrender its position as the world's leader, forgo its role as chief promoter and defender of democracy, and give up on over seventy years of collective action to preserve freedom and civil liberties around the world.

Our nation's democratic principles and ideals are under attack by a kleptocratic Russian regime sowing divisions amongst the American public and Western society through information warfare. Russia's strategic motto is "divided we stand, divided we fall". It's time the United States remind the world, that despite our day-to-day policy debates and political squabbles, we stand united, alongside our allies, in defending our democratic

---

https://www.buzzfeed.com/craigsilverman/viral-fake-election-news-outperformed-real-news-on-facebook?utm_term=.etYEzgQno#.im3kXQAKR

[15] Olivia Solon and Julia Carrie Wong (16 December 2016) *Facebook's plan to tackle fake news raises questions over limitations.* The Guardian. Available at: https://www.theguardian.com/technology/2016/dec/16/facebook-fake-news-system-problems-fact-checking

[16] Clint Watts and Andrew Weisburd (22 January 2017) *Can the Michelen Model Fix Fake News?* Daily Beast. Available at: http://www.thedailybeast.com/articles/2017/01/22/can-the-michelin-model-fix-fake-news.html

[17] Kathy Frankovic (14 December 2016) *Americans and Trump part ways over Russia.* YouGov. Available at: https://today.yougov.com/news/2016/12/14/americans-and-trump-part-ways-over-russia/

system of government from the meddling of power-hungry tyrants and repressive authoritarians that prey on their people and suppress humanity.

Chairman BURR. Mr. Watts, thank you for your testimony, and all written testimony will be included as part of the record.

The Chair and the Vice Chairman are going to exit and vote. I'm going to recognize Senator Risch for his questions and in our absence he'll allow back and forth based upon seniority.

Senator Risch.

Senator RISCH [presiding]. Thank you, Mr. Chairman.

Gentlemen, it always impresses me the fact that when we hear people talking about Russian policy and what they want, first of all, how uniform it is. Everybody seems to agree on where they're going, what they do and what they're doing to get there. But after processing that over a long period of time, one's got to come to the thought process of what happens in a post-Putin Russia, because everyone's got a shelf life and his has been extended, it looks to me, well beyond what normally would happen under these circumstances.

So give me your thoughts briefly, each of you, if you would, as to what happens? Do they stay on the same track they're on or do they come to the realization that there's bigger and better things in life to pursue than what they're doing right now?

Mr. Godson.

Dr. GODSON. Well, thank you for the question. As you know, there are a lot of variables here at work. One would be what we—how we respond to Putin and the behavior of the apparatus that they have. Do we let them continue to do this or do we start to develop some sort of a strategic response to that? That would be one of the variables.

Do they find that they can get away with, use activities as they have in the past? And if so, then the elite that has taken power in Russia would be inclined to continue. They found that even when they sometimes have not been as effective as they expected, that active measures still is a capability that enables them to—I use the example of being able to fight above their economic and political capabilities.

So unless there was a dramatic change in the regime, there's little reason to believe that they would cease the active measures policy and strategy they have, barring that we don't actually cauterize it and limit its effectiveness. If we don't, then they'll have an incentive to continue.

Senator RISCH. Dr. Rumer.

Dr. RUMER. Thank you, sir. Well, Mr. Putin I believe is 62, a man in his prime. He's positioned to run in 2018 again for another six-year term. So I think what we see today is going to be with us for a long time, by the looks of it for the next two presidential terms in this country. So we should base our policy accordingly.

I think it would be incorrect and counterproductive to tar all Russians with the same brush. But there's something there in Russian traditional security perceptions that transcends party lines, that transcends regimes, and Russian perceptions of security don't really change all that much over time. So I think we should be thinking about the drivers of Russian foreign and security policy in terms of continuity rather than radical change. After all, we already saw radical change in 1991 and things in the end didn't really change that much.

As long as Russian elites will see themselves—as long as they see themselves as being inferior and struggling against a more advanced and a more powerful Western alliance, they will be relying on all tools in their toolkit, and information warfare will be—disinformation will be part of it.

We may hope that if some day someone like the corruption fighter Alexei Navalny gets elected, rises to the leadership of the country, having been a victim of such disinformation, he may be more restrained in it. But I would say that the basic parameters of Russian policy are generally set in place.

Senator RISCH. Thank you, Doctor. I've only got a short time left. I want to hear from Mr. Watts.

Mr. WATTS. Regarding Mr. Putin, I would look to these two gentlemen primarily. But my thoughts are: one, he's not going away any time soon; two, he will definitely shape some sort of a successor in his place to continue on with what he's doing right now.

I think the third big thing that we can't discount is the connection with criminality. There is—between these elites and their sort of predatory capitalist practices, what we see in cyberspace with cybercrime and how they've used hackers very well as part of their active measures, we can't discount that we'll see a predatory elite emerge that will be something we have to deal with.

I think the fourth thing, which goes to the first point, is I'm not sure what our policy or stance is with regards to Russia at this point in the United States. I think that's the number one thing we have to figure out, because that will shape how they interface with us. Having watched the end of the Soviet Union as a cadet at West Point and then fast forwarding to today, I'm a little bit lost as to what our U.S. interests are or how they're coalescing. I know what I would recommend, but I think that will have a major impact on how we will be able to interface. And maybe I see opportunity in Putin's departure.

Senator RISCH. Thank you, Mr. Watts.

Senator Feinstein.

Senator FEINSTEIN. Thank you, Senator Risch.

Gentlemen, thank you very much for being here and thank you for your testimony. I'm sorry I was out to vote while I missed some of it. But I've been on this committee for 16 years and the intelligence community report, which is the report of all of our major intelligence agencies which was released on January 6th, is among the strongest I've read. It covers the motivation and the scope of Russia's actions regarding our elections, as well as the cyber tools and the media campaigns they used to influence public opinion.

The report makes a key judgment and here it is: "Russian President Vladimir Putin ordered an influence campaign in 2016 aimed at the United States political election, the consistent goals of which were to undermine public faith in the United States' democratic process, denigrate Secretary Clinton and harm her electability and potential presidency."

It further assesses that, and these are quotes: "Putin and the Russian government developed a clear preference for President-elect Trump."

Here's two questions. Do you believe the Intelligence Community Assessment accurately characterized the goals of Russian influence activities in the election? And I'd like to go down the line with a yes or no answer. If you want to explain it, that would be fine. Who would like to go first?

Dr. GODSON. Thank you for a difficult question. I personally don't find myself at odds with the ICA study that you identified However, the statement that this was developed in 2016 needs to be parsed a bit. The Russians could not do this if they started in 2016. They wouldn't have had the capability. In the active measures world, one can want to do many things, but one has to have the means to do this.

Senator FEINSTEIN. When would you estimate it was started by your statement?

Dr. GODSON. Well, it's not that I have a specific date, but that one needs to have an infrastructure abroad to be able to do this. Now, you can use some of the infrastructure in your own country, especially with cyber capabilities, but——

Senator FEINSTEIN. Which they had.

Dr. GODSON. Which they had. But active measures usually involve people as well as machines. And it would be extraordinary if they hadn't prepared a lot of the ground to be able to do this, not only in the United States, but in other countries as well. They have this apparatus, and this apparatus is well-staffed, well-trained.

The training of the people who work in this apparatus is quite surprising to us. We've known about it, but we don't really take it very seriously. It's not three months or six months training or a year's training. They have much longer training periods and some of them are pretty good, not ten feet tall, of course, but pretty good.

Senator FEINSTEIN. I got the point.

Next person.

Dr. RUMER. Yes.

Senator FEINSTEIN. Thank you. I appreciate it.

Mr. WATTS. Yes, and I can give you the timeline of their development if you would like.

Senator FEINSTEIN. Please.

Vice Chairman WARNER. We have accounts dating back to 2009 that are tied to active measures. 2014 was their capability development based on my assessment, where they started working on their influence campaigns. 2015 was when they tied hacking and influence together for the first time, specifically during the DNC breaches. I was notified in November of 2015 that I had been targeted by a cyber attack.

2016 was the push into the U.S. audience landscape to build audience. August 2016 was when I witnessed them pushing toward the election and that was in full—or August of 2015 all the way through 2016, so a one-year buildup to the election.

Senator FEINSTEIN. Thank you.

Has Russia ever—I think I know the answer to this, but if you would elaborate on it—conducted other similar campaigns in other countries to this level of impact with the goal of tilting the playing field to increase one candidate's chance of winning?

Mr. Watts, if you'd go first.

Mr. WATTS. Yes. I believe you need to look back to 2014 in both Ukraine and another Eastern European country that's escaping me. In 2015, 2016, the Brexit campaign should be examined. I can't prove it one way or another. And then today, all of the European elections that they're choosing to meddle in—France, Germany, Netherlands, Czech Republic.

Senator FEINSTEIN. Thank you.

Would you like to respond?

Dr. RUMER. Yes, they have conducted such campaigns in Ukraine in 2004 and in 2014 in Georgia. They have intervened heavily in domestic political campaigns in the Baltic States. So there are ample examples of that.

Senator FEINSTEIN. Thank you.

Would you please respond, Doctor?

Dr. GODSON. Yes, they have a history of doing this well before this and they find it a successful use of their resources. So it does not surprise.

Senator RISCH. Thank you, Doctor. Thank you, Senator Feinstein.

Senator Rubio.

Senator RUBIO. Thank you.

Thank you all for being here. I'm concerned that in our inquiry—and I certainly think it's important for us to know what happened—we are focusing so much on the tactics that we're not focusing on the broader strategy that's at play here. I want to briefly go through a number of instances and have the panel comment on whether or not they believe these are indicative of the efforts that are being targeted against the United States and the rest of the world by Vladimir Putin.

We all know that Angela Merkel has taken a tough line on Ukraine against Russia. We know that there's a lot of controversy in Germany around migrants. In early 2016, a 13-year-old known only as "Lisa S.," a dual Russian-German citizen whose family had moved to Germany from Russia in 2004, told police she had been kidnapped in East Berlin by what appeared to be Middle Eastern migrants and raped for over 30 hours. There was outrage in Germany and, obviously, protests against Merkel.

The Russian foreign minister almost immediately jumped on the story, talking about the need to defend "our" Lisa, quote-unquote, and of course this story was spread far and wide by Russian-speaking entities and Russian media outlets.

Subsequently, the prosecutors in Berlin announced that they had clear evidence that during those 30 hours she was missing, Lisa S. was actually in fact with people that she knew and a medical examination showed that she had not been the victim of a rape.

Earlier this year, a little-known news outlet published on a website an article that claimed that the United States was deploying 3,600 tanks to Eastern Europe to prepare for war with Russia. 3,600 tanks would represent about 40 percent of our entire tank force. Within days the story was republished by dozens of outlets in the United States and throughout Europe. As it turns out, the truth is we deployed 87 tanks.

There is—going all the way back to September 11, 2015, residents in Louisiana awoke to a message, many of them did, on their Twitter feed that said: "Toxic fume hazard warning in this area until 1:30 p.m. Take shelter, check local media and ColumbiaChemical.com."

On Twitter accounts, there were hundreds of accounts documenting a disaster right down the road from the people. One account said: "A powerful explosion heard from miles away at a chemical plant in Centerville, Louisiana," a man named John Merritt tweeted. @AnnaRoussella shared an image of flames engulfing the plant. @Quesera12 posted a video of surveillance footage from the local gas station capturing the explosion. Another Twitter account posted a screenshot of CNN's home page showing the story had already made national news, claiming that ISIS had claimed credit for the attack, according to one YouTube video.

A woman named @Zopakdon9—Anna Clinton McLaren is her name, I guess—tweeted to Karl Rove: "Karl, is this really ISIS responsible for the #ColumbiaChemicals? Tell Obama we should bomb Iraq."

If anyone had taken the trouble to check CNN, as this article in The New York Times outlined, there was no such attack. It was a hoax, not some simple prank, as the article goes on to say, but a highly coordinated disinformation campaign involving dozens of fake accounts that posted hundreds of tweets for hours, targeting a list of figures precisely chosen to generate maximum attention.

"The perpetrators didn't just doctor screen shots from CNN"—and I'm reading from the New York Times article—"they also created functional clones of the websites of the Louisiana TV stations and the like."

The list goes on and on. We should fully document it in our report to the American people. A false story spreading, claiming that Germany's oldest church had been burned down by a thousand Muslims chanting "Allah Akbar." Another story claiming that the European Union was planning to ban snowmen as racist.

All of this, and on and on, and we should begin to document them for the American people. Isn't this the larger problem? Let me rephrase that. Aren't we in the midst of a blitzkrieg, for lack of a better term, of informational warfare conducted by Russian trolls under the command of Vladimir Putin, designed to sow instability, pit us against each other as Americans?

This same article—I don't have enough time—it goes on: They posted false stories about a police shooting in Atlanta that never happened, about a series of things. In essence, are we in danger here because we are focused on the very important tactical move that happened in the election of 2016, to miss the broader point, and that is that this is a coordinated effort across multiple spectrums to sow instability and to pit Americans against one another politically, socioeconomically, demographically, and the like?

Mr. WATTS. I think the two lines of effort you brought up there that the Russians use are social dynamics that they play on, ethnic divisions, and global calamity or inciting fear. These two lines haven't been discussed much. The third one is financial. They oftentimes put out fake stories about U.S. companies, which then cause stock dips, which allow all sorts of predatory trading and other things to happen.

We've focused on disinformation around the political scene. But misinformation across the board, particularly from the Russian propaganda networks, has incited fear inside the United States on multiple occasions, as you noted. One last year was there was the

JFK Terminal shutdown about alleged gunshots. We watched social media trolls and gray outlets pump fake stories out which ramped up that fear, which caused mass panic.

So they have created the ability, by gaining audience in the United States, to steer Americans unwittingly in many difficult directions that can cause all sorts of danger and even violence in certain cases. I think the Pizzagate scandal that we saw last fall is another such example of misinformation, maybe not attributed to Russia, but we have a problem writ large right now with our information sources.

Senator RISCH. Senator Rubio, do you want to——

Senator RUBIO. No, I want to listen.

Dr. GODSON. I think you hit the nail on the head and I don't really have a lot to add to it. We are faced with a strategic attack. It's not a kinetic attack usually. It's a political attack. Then the question comes what sort of strategic response are we going to be able to develop to that, that attack? We could elaborate on that.

Senator RISCH. Senator Warner.

Vice Chairman WARNER. Again, I thank all the witnesses for the testimony.

Dr. Rumer, I'm going to start with you. We've heard a lot recently about the role of Oleg Deripaska, the head of Russia's largest aluminum company, and the role he may have played in helping to support the goals of President Putin. Can you characterize Mr. Deripaska's role in this area? And then more broadly, are there any of the oligarchs in Russia, at least those not in exile, that aren't somehow caught up in the Kremlin's foreign policy activities? Are there any of them that are truly independent?

Dr. RUMER. Thank you, Senator Warner. I can't add anything to the conversation about Mr. Deripaska beyond what's appeared in the public domain. I don't think I have any special insights here. I feed off the same reporting that's appeared in the papers.

I would be careful to describe all Russian oligarchs—and "oligarch" itself is a fairly ill-defined term. It was prominent once, but it's a much bigger class of major Russian businessmen.

I would be reluctant to describe them all as tools of the Kremlin. Obviously, Russian businessmen who do business in Russia have to be mindful of Kremlin political preferences and the Kremlin has considerable influence over them. But I don't have—I can't speak from concrete information about them being directly instruments of the Kremlin foreign policy. That's not something that I have evidence to back up.

So I think I'll stop at that.

Vice Chairman WARNER. Mr. Watts, one of the things in your testimony—I've been talking a lot about the use of the internet trolls and their ability to then exponentially gain more power through creating these botnets. I'd love you to kind of comment about what we can do to preclude that on a going-forward basis, and perhaps you can explain this technique better than I have in my various public statements.

Mr. WATTS. Sure. The first thing that I think we need to understand is it's not all automated and it's not all human. There's a combination of the two. So you have a series of humans that work in their psychological warfare groups, that command both bots at the same time. I like to, as an analogy, to look at it like artillery. You have someone who's engaging with you as an individual and at the same time they can launch a bot to amplify that story forward.

Vice Chairman WARNER. Obviously, a "bot" is the ability for a computer to take over other computers that are not being used and in effect magnify the number of hits they might get to a particular social media site, correct?

Mr. WATTS. Exactly. Or you can create more personas in Twitter, for example, which makes it look like there are more people than there really are. It's a Potemkin village strategy essentially that amplifies your appearance.

So what they do is they launch those simultaneously as they begin the engagement or push of false news stories, usually from RT and Sputnik News. They do that in unison, which games the social media system such that such a high volume of content being pushed at the same time raises that into the trends that you'll see.

If you look at Facebook or Twitter or whatever it might be, you'll see the top ten stories that are out right now. It pushes that up there. As soon as it pushes that into that top ten feed, mainstream media outlets then are watching that and they start to examine that content.

So, for example, the Incirlik attack I talked about, one of the key hashtags they pushed is #Media. The goal is to get that into the top of Twitter streams so that mainstream media has to respond to that story. When mainstream media responds to it or just looks at it without even commenting on it, it takes over organically and you'll see it move around the internet like a virus.

Vice Chairman WARNER. One thing—and I'm going to spend a lot of time on this this afternoon—there have been reports that their ability to target this information, some reports at least, saying that in the last week of the campaign in certain precincts in Wisconsin, Michigan, and Pennsylvania, there was so much misinformation coming out talking about Hillary Clinton's illnesses or Hillary Clinton stealing money from the State Department, that it completely blanked out any of the back and forth that was actually going on in the campaign.

One of the things that seems curious is, would the Russians on their own have that level of sophisticated knowledge about the American political system if they didn't at least get some advice from someone in America?

Mr. WATTS. Yes. I know this from working on influence campaigns in the counterterrorism context. If you do an appropriate target audience analysis on social media, you can actually identify an audience in a foreign country or in the United States, parse out all of their preferences. Part of the reason those bios had "conservative," "Christian," "America," all those terms in it, is those are the most common ones. If you inhale all the accounts of people in Wisconsin, you identify the most common terms in it, you just recreate accounts that look exactly like people from Wisconsin.

So that way, whenever you're trying to socially engineer them and convince them that the information is true, it's much more simple because you see somebody and they look exactly like you, even down to the pictures. When you look at the pictures, it looks like an American from the Midwest or the South or Wisconsin or whatever the location is.

And they will change those. They can reprogram them. Where they tend to show their hand is, the problem is once they build an audience they don't want to get rid of it. So you'll see them build an audience and try and influence one segment, let's say of the English-speaking media, and then they will reprogram it to try and influence a different story. It's the same problem any cable news outlet would have. Once you build an audience and you change your content to some other topic, you still want to keep your old audience or otherwise you can't gain any traction.

Vice Chairman WARNER. Again, my time is up, but I just want to know: This can be used—it was used in 2016 toward one candidate, but obviously Russia's interests are Russia's interests.

Mr. WATTS. Well, it's used right now against people on both sides of the aisle. We will watch them play both sides. They might go after a Republican person in this room tomorrow and then they'll switch. It's solely based on what they want to achieve in their own landscape, whatever the Russian foreign policy objectives are.

So if they want to achieve one candidate—let's say President Trump, for example, wins and now turns against them; they will turn on President Trump as well. They will play—they win because they play both sides, and the audience will go with them once they have them.

Chairman BURR [presiding]. I do know that the Vice Chairman hates Russia, just to make that public.

Senator Collins.

Senator COLLINS. Thank you, Mr. Chairman.

Dr. Godson, you make the point that the Russians don't always win with their active measures and you mentioned the period of the 1940s and the 1950s. In your judgment, how successful have the Russians been in the last year in achieving their goal of sowing doubt, polarization, and trying to disrupt and cast doubt on the validity of the election, putting aside the issue for the moment of the critical question of whether there was any collusion between any campaign and the Russian efforts?

Dr. GODSON. From the information that we have in the public sector and the private sector, I would say that they must be rather pleased with the results of their investment, whenever they started to develop this campaign.

I think, though, however, they—and the fact is that they are seeming to prepare to do the same thing in other campaigns abroad. So looking at the way they've behaved over the long course of time that they've used active measures, I think they will continue to do this and to reap some benefits from it, unless there is a considerable response from the democratic societies. At the moment, I would say that our response is too restrained and that, unless they see that there is a cost to this that makes this not a very attractive thing to do, I don't see why they won't continue it.

I hope that's responsive.

Senator COLLINS. Thank you.

Dr. Rumer, Mr. Watts made the point that the Russians will go after either side, that they're trying to disrupt society, cast doubt on Western democracies. One largely overlooked part of the Intelligence Committee's—the intelligence community's report last fall was information in the annex that suggested that Russia Today, which most people view as an organ of the Russian government, was instrumental in trying to advance the protests of Occupy Wall Street.

Could you comment on that, and is that an example of Russia working to promote the far left versus the far right that we hear so much about?

Dr. RUMER. Yes, ma'am. It's a perfect example in that Occupy Wall Street was a genuine movement on the left, but it certainly serves the interests of Russian propaganda to play it up as a major challenge, as something representing a major fault line in our society, because it drives the message that the United States is in decline, the United States is in crisis, plays up to audiences at home in Russia and abroad that the United States is not the perfect society, something that they really like to emphasize.

So that's an excellent example and I think it deserves the attention, the spotlight that you cast on it. Mr. Watts referred to the minor protest outside our base in Incirlik in Turkey. Well, there's another example, that there was a protest, but again it's blown out of all proportions.

As you know, the best propaganda is that which has a grain of truth to it and then gets played up and up and up.

Senator COLLINS. Thank you, Mr. Chairman.

Chairman BURR. Senator Wyden.

Senator WYDEN. Thank you, Mr. Chairman.

Let me say thank you to our witnesses. Gentlemen, here's where we are now. The American people are worried about what's ahead with regard to Russia. The public now gets most of its information from leaks, from daily press stories, and apparently inaccurate tweets from the President.

This feeds distrust and causes Americans to question the legitimacy of our government. So I believe the committee needs to lift the fog of secrecy about what really happened to our democracy. That's why it's so important we have open hearings with the intelligence community, the FBI, Homeland Security, and Treasury.

I believe the key to a successful investigation is following the money. Yesterday I wrote a letter to the Chairman and the Vice Chair urging the committee to look into any and all financial relationships between Russia and Donald Trump and his associates.

I'm also taking this issue on as the Ranking Member of the Finance Committee, of which Senator Burr and Senator Warner are also members. I and other members of the Finance Committee have already urged that the committee exercise its authority to obtain and review Donald Trump's tax returns. This review ought to include the Trump Organization and its partnerships.

Senate investigators should also look into any violations of the Foreign Corrupt Practices Act, which ensures that investors are not paying bribes overseas. The Treasury Department is responsible for other programs and investigations that may uncover suspicious financial activities by Donald Trump and his associates.

It is already a matter of public record that entities associated with Donald Trump have been the subject of millions of dollars of fines for willful, repeated, and longstanding violations of anti-money-laundering laws. Information about Donald Trump's finances, his family, and his associates may lead to Russia. We know that in 2008 the President's son said that "Russians make up a pretty disproportionate cross section of a lot of our assets." Since then, we've gotten mostly smoke and mirrors.

The committee needs to follow the money wherever it leads, because if money-laundering, corruption of any kind, or fishy real estate deals point to the Russian oligarchs and criminal elements, then the Russian government may only be a step or two away from us.

So now my question. There is an extraordinary history of money-laundering in Russia. Billions of dollars from corruption and other illegal activities have been moved out of the country. What that means is that Russia's corruption problem may also be our corruption problem.

So here's my question for the three of you as experts on Russia. I'd like you three to tell us about corruption in Russia so as to help us follow the money in our investigation.

Here's my specific question. I'm going to start with you, Mr. Watts. How can the committee track this fuzzy line between the Russian oligarchs, Russian organized crime, and the Russian government?

Mr. WATTS. Thank you, Senator. I would first start off with, I'm not the foremost Russian expert. I came to this through the Islamic State and ISIS. I'm really a counterterrorism person for the most part and came to active measures mostly because active measures came after me.

The second part that I would add to this discussion, though, is there is a money trail to be searched for and discovered. We've focused very heavily on elites in our public discussion, what are elite people doing. But this influence action has both a virtual component and a physical component that's happened.

I would say that what I can't see which I would want to know is: What is happening in Eastern Europe? There's a disproportionate number of fake news outlets, conspiratorial websites, that are run from there, that are English-speaking editors that are pro-Russian, trained in Russia sometimes. How are they funded? That would be one component.

My guess or my estimate, my hypothesis working in the intelligence field, is that there is some sort of Russian intel asset that is funding them in one way or another through some sort of scheme.

The other part that I think we should be looking at is follow the trail of dead Russians. There's been more dead Russians in the past three months that are tied to this investigation, who have assets in banks all over the world. They are dropping dead even in Western countries. We've seen arrests in I believe it's Spain and different computer security companies that are based in Russia which provide services to the United States.

These are all huge openings to understand how they are funded by the Russian government. I don't have the capability to do that from where I sit, but I think that's a huge angle. If you can prove that part of it, I have to say on the influence side of it we can see it.

The one thing that's been misconstrued in the public discussion about Russian influence is that it's covert. You can hack stuff and be covert, but you can't influence and be covert. You have to ultimately show your hand. That's why we've been able to discover it online.

But the missing part is how did they conduct this influence. There are newspapers, there are media outlets. The Balkans are littered right now with these sorts of outlets. That's where I would start to dig in the financial space.

Senator WYDEN. I'm almost out of time. Dr. Rumer, same thing. This fuzzy line is what I'm particularly interested in: organized crime, oligarchs, and the government. I heard you talk about one person, you couldn't comment on him. But just give me your analysis about this fuzzy line, because I keep coming back to that.

Dr. RUMER. It is definitely a fuzzy line, and I think those relationships are probably best discussed not in an open session, because——

Senator WYDEN. You're saying they ought to be discussed?

Dr. RUMER. I believe they ought to be discussed.

Senator WYDEN. Good. Fair enough.

Dr. RUMER. But I do believe that it is something for our intelligence community to take up rather than for us to discuss in open session.

Senator WYDEN. I probably ought to quit while I'm ahead——

Chairman BURR. Senator Blunt.

Senator WYDEN. Mr. Chairman, can Mr. Godson just finish that question?

Chairman BURR. Dr. Godson, quickly.

Dr. GODSON. I'm very pleased——

Chairman BURR. Turn your mike on.

Dr. GODSON. I'm very pleased that you're having this open session. I think it's very useful. But I do think that this is a sensitive subject and so that it will require skill and care on the part of our society so we don't overreact, which in our history we sometimes have, to being surprised. So I do think there should be a time to discuss this.

Senator WYDEN. Thank you, Mr. Chairman.

Chairman BURR. Senator Blunt.

Senator BLUNT. Thank you, Chair.

Dr. Godson, let's just start right there. Why do you think we— I've got about four questions, so they don't need to be exhaustive, and I can follow up with more written questions later. And, Mr. Watts, I'm going to come to you next.

Why do you think there was this element of surprise? I mean, this is not new Russian activity in other places in the world. I think Mr. Watts said they had to start before 2016. But it does seem that the intel community, the U.S. Government, the media, is surprised that they have this level of involvement. You just said we shouldn't have been surprised. Why do you think we were surprised?

Dr. GODSON. I do think it has something to do with our culture, that we don't expect people to behave in this particular way. We've been surprised many times in our history, so I don't think——

Senator BLUNT. We expect them to do it everywhere else, but not do it here?

Dr. GODSON. Well, we just are sort of surprised when somebody takes a concerted effort to be involved in our affairs. We know that sometimes this happens abroad, but we don't really think this is a major tool or instrument that people use. So we found ourselves surprised in the 1940s and the 1970s and the 1980s and so on.

So I'm not too surprised we are surprised.

Senator BLUNT. Mr. Watts, why do you think we seem to have been so unready for this?

Mr. WATTS. One, our intelligence community has been over-focused on terrorism and the Islamic State and there wasn't much resources or bandwidth to focus on it. The second one is our traditional methods for detecting and counter-intelligence, things like active measures, are based on HUMINTs. We run spies versus counter-spies. Most of this influence came online. They essentially duplicated the old active measures system without setting foot inside the United States.

I think the third part of it is the intel community in the United States is very biased against open source information. They've been surprised repeatedly: ISIS, the Arab Spring. You can go back over the past six to seven years. We worry a lot about security clearances and badges and who gets access to doors and does the break room have a shredder, but when it comes to the open source we miss what's right in front of our nose.

My two colleagues and I use three laptops and we do this at our house. But for some reason the entire intel apparatus, with billions of dollars, will miss a tweet or a Facebook post that's right in front of them, but will be highly focused on the security system and these closed sources, which are super-useful. But we have not changed that orientation in our intel community.

Senator BLUNT. Mr. Rumer, in Europe do you think the interventions there were so obviously different that we wouldn't have caught on? Or how do you see the difference in what the Russians have done, particularly in the past 15 years, in Europe and what they did here?

Dr. RUMER. Well, there was an element of unpreparedness on our part, I agree with my colleagues. I would say that—well, I can speak from personal experience and that is I just didn't believe that any one intervention, any one agent, can swing our election across 50 states. I think—I thought nobody in their right mind would try to take on the challenge of such expensive complexity.

But then when you think about it more carefully, as we have now with the benefit of hindsight, if you look at the election of 2000, when the Florida vote was decided by a very small number of votes, when we now know some of the votes were decided—some states were decided by a very small margin—you realize that a more sophisticated actor that has, as my colleagues have pointed out, years and decades of experience of playing in this field, can actually aspire to make a meaningful difference.

Senator BLUNT. Let me ask another question about that. I know the Vice Chairman mentioned hand-counting of ballots in the recent elections in one European country. You said that the Russian intelligence services directly intervened. We don't have any reason to believe—any of you can answer this—that they intervened in any election counting system this time? I think we should be concerned that that never be allowed to happen and one of our goals here should be to be sure we're protecting that part of the process.

But when you said directly intervened in the elections, no indication, Mr. Rumer, of directly intervening anywhere in the counting of votes on election day?

Dr. RUMER. Right. There are public statements from our intelligence community and law enforcement and DHS that our counting systems have not been affected. I can only go on the strength of that and I fully believe that statement. But we certainly should be aware of that and concerned about it.

Senator BLUNT. Absolutely.

Thank you, Mr. Chairman.

Chairman BURR. Senator Heinrich.

Senator HEINRICH. Thank you, Chairman.

I want to start out by just thanking the Chairman and the Vice Chairman for their willingness to work so closely together on leading this investigation. I certainly think that today's hearing is helpful in setting a baseline for the intentions and the techniques of Russia's active measures campaigns. But I also look forward to public hearings in which we can dig even deeper into the substance of what happened specifically in the 2016 election.

Similarly, I believe it's critical that we dig into the financial aspects involved and that we follow the money to determine whether and how the Russians have used financial leverage to achieve their strategic goals. I think we need to do everything possible to get to the truth. The American people certainly deserve no less, and I think if we do not take this seriously it is not hyperbolic to say that our fundamental democratic institutions are at risk.

Dr. Godson said something in his statement for the record about the history of relying on agents of influence. In other words, recruiting and coopting sympathetic groups or individuals in the U.S. and in the West to advance the Russian agenda. Do you all agree that financing is one of the methods often used by Russia to recruit sympathetic agents?

Dr. GODSON. Yes.

Dr. RUMER. Yes. There is publicly available evidence of a Moscow-based bank financing one of the presidential candidates in France.

Senator HEINRICH. When they use financial resources to recruit agents of influence, like the example you just made, is it always a simple exchange of money for assistance or does Russia sometimes attempt to buy influence more subtly, through access to lucrative business deals and contracts and those kinds of arrangements?

Dr. GODSON. Yes, I think all of the above we can show examples of in the past.

Dr. RUMER. Yes, they have used their considerable financial business leverage in Eastern Europe to cut favorable energy deals, to offer lucrative deals to local companies and governments.

Mr. WATTS. I think the key point—and this is comparing it to Soviet active measures today—is we didn't do business transactions with the Soviet Union. So they have so many more access points to compromise people financially or to influence them on the financial space that they couldn't have done during the Cold War.

Senator HEINRICH. This next question is for any of you. I'm curious if you see money in politics as an opening for Russia to be able to potentially manipulate our elections, especially given their expertise at moving financial resources through networks and the change in our own environment, in which there is now a lack of transparency in the current U.S. campaign finance environment, where oftentimes you have elections where a majority of the dollars spent are not even originating from the individual candidates themselves.

Have any of you given that some thought?

Mr. WATTS. I think it's a little bit overstated, based on the public part of it. The Russians aren't stupid. They know that if they are ever caught directly putting money into what looks like a Manchurian candidate kind of scenario, this could be provocation for war or it could be sanctions. It could be a host of different things.

At the same point, I would also offer you, from an intelligence perspective, why not look at it as a way to compromise somebody? So if you have a candidate that's doing well and you have very open campaign finance, why not slip them some money where they don't know the original source of it, such that if it's revealed later they are discredited?

So it can go both ways. It's not just promotion. It can also be used as a tool and a weapon.

Senator HEINRICH. You, Mr. Watts, I think did a really good job of laying out for us how these influence operations actually have the impact of sort of organically changing the trends on media and end up being sort of a self-reinforcing mechanism.

Are there analytic or digital tools that can discount the impact of those bots and of that manufactured forcing mechanism within the way that information travels on the web today and impacts the media?

Mr. WATTS. I think all the social media companies are starting to realize that their ad revenue mechanisms can be manipulated for this. There is more than just Russian fake news out there. You've got profiteers, you've got political groups that do that, and you've got satire, which is thrown in the mix of it.

You're seeing the social media companies now try and regulate this now or deem things as fake news, but that's going to fail. Ultimately, any attempt to deem things as fake or not fake is going to lead to freedom of speech violations, freedom of the press violations, because how do you do that? How do you determine who's being fair or not.

I think a better way to do it and what we propose is to create the version of Information Consumer Reports, which is an independent agency which is funded by the social media companies, has no government involvement, no government funding, that provides a rating in terms of the news that shows up on your feed, such that, much like nutrition labels on food, you know what you're consuming.

Right now part of the reason this is so effective is a fake news outlet can pop up one day, pump out stories that are sensational, and fall down the next. The consumer and American on their

Facebook feed, which is curated to the things that they like to click on, and even in their Google searches, which is curated to things other people like to click on like them, end up clicking on these things because they're popular.

If they had a score or a rating, some sort of symbol there, that said, you're more than welcome to click on this, but this is the National Enquirer, you can evaluate how much of it is truth and how much is manipulated truth and how much is false—just like we saw with Consumer Reports when I was growing up, it had 15 variables, it's rated over time, and it becomes a trusted entity that you can go to.

I think that's a better way to do it. We're not restricting Americans' freedom of speech and press, and at the same point if they want to look at fake news they can look at it, but they know what they're getting into.

Senator HEINRICH. Thank you, Mr. Chair.

Chairman BURR. Senator Lankford.

Senator LANKFORD. It's hard to believe we're even having this hearing today discussing this topic, since Putin already cleared this up earlier today. He came out with a public statement just hours ago saying: "Watch my lips. No." and then followed up with: "All these things are fictional, illusory, provocations, lies, used for domestic American political agendas. The anti-Russian card is played by different political forces inside the United States to trade on and consolidate their positions inside."

Well, he's certainly consolidated us.

It is painful to watch the Russian people trapped in a regime that is doing this worldwide. They'd like to be able to watch the Olympics and know their athletes weren't doped ahead of time. They would like to believe their own news when the Russians proclaim, we're not in Ukraine and we're not in Syria, and they are. And it would be nice if we could, as he said, "Watch my lips" and know that he's not trying to deceive our audiences.

My question is, first: Why did he think he could get away with it this time? This is not new for the Russians. They've done this for a long time across Europe. But he was much more engaged this time in our election. Why now?

Mr. Watts.

Mr. WATTS. I think this answer is very simple and is what no one is really saying in this room, which is: Part of the reason active measures have worked in this U.S. election is because the Commander-in-Chief has used Russian active measures at times against his opponents. On 14 August 2016, his campaign chairman, after a debunked——

Senator LANKFORD. When you say "his," who's "his"?

Mr. WATTS. Paul Manafort cited the fake Incirlik story as a terrorist attack on CNN, and he used it as a talking point.

On 11 October, President Trump stood on a stage and cited what appears to be a fake news story from Sputnik News, that disappeared from the internet. He denies the intel from the United States about Russia. He claimed that the election could be rigged. That was the number one theme pushed by RT, Sputnik News, white outlets all the way up until the election. He's made claims of voter fraud, that President Obama's not a citizen, that Congressman Cruz is not a citizen.

So part of the reason active measures works and it does today in terms of Trump Tower being wiretapped is because they parrot the same lines. So Putin is correct, he can say that he's not influencing anything because he's just putting out his stance. But until we get a firm basis on fact and fiction in our own country, get some agreement about the facts, whether it be do I support the intelligence community or a story I read on my Twitter feed, we're going to have a big problem.

I can tell you right now today, gray outlets that are Soviet-pushing accounts, tweet at President Trump during high volumes when they know he's online and they push conspiracy theories. So if he is to click on one of those or cite one of those, it just proves Putin correct that, we can use this as a lever against the Americans.

Senator LANKFORD. So this started in 2008, 2009 time period, as you've cited before with your previous timeline. Even before this rose up, even when there were 16 Republican candidates on the stage, this was a long time coming and it seemed to be very well organized this time.

Part of my question is, I get that completely; why this time? They looked to be more prepared—probing, evaluating states, trying to get into voter records, trying to be more active in the process.

Mr. WATTS. They have plausible deniability. If you wanted to run this during the Cold War, you would have had to put agents inside the United States. They would have been stalked by counter-intelligence professionals. They would have been run down. You couldn't have gained an audience on a communist newspaper, for example.

Today you can create the content, gain the audience, build the bots, pick out the election and even the voters that are valued the most in swing states, and actually insert the right content in a deliberate period. They pre-planned it. They were based a year and a half out. They're doing it today on the European elections.

Here's the other thing that needs to come up. They try all messages. You know, we've been very focused on our presidential election. The Republicans tend to come up. But the Democrats, they were there, too. They were with Bernie Sanders supporters, trying to influence them in different directions.

So they play all sides. Much like I learned in infantry school about how they use artillery, they fire artillery everywhere and once they get a break in the wall that's where they swarm in and they focus. So they do that very well today.

You'll see them in Europe supporting people on the left or right, whichever will dismantle the democratic function that they're after. So I think the important point moving forward is we have to educate our public and even our institutions.

And the mainstream media is right to be taking some on the chin right now. They've fallen for a lot of these fake news stories. They've amplified it and they've not gone back and done good fact-checking. The media needs to improve. Our U.S. Government institutions need to improve, and we've got to help Americans understand what the facts are, because if we don't we are lost. We will become two separate, maybe three, separate worlds in the United States, just because of this little bitty pinprick that was put in by a foreign country.

Senator LANKFORD. Which is their goal.

On that, Mr. Chairman, I yield back.

Chairman BURR. Senator Manchin.

Senator MANCHIN. Mr. Chairman, thank you so much.

I want to thank Senator King for allowing me. I have another meeting I've got to attend. But I wanted to ask this question.

I've been around long enough to remember that my school desk at home protected me if I jumped underneath of it and held my head during a nuclear attack from Russia. I'm not sure that my United States Senate desk if I jump underneath of it and hold my head will protect me this time, and that's putting it mildly.

With that being said, much has been written about the new hybrid style of warfare practiced by the Russians recently in Georgia, Crimea, and Ukraine. To be brief, Russia believes the lines between war and peace are blurred. Wars are no longer declared and no longer fought in the traditional manner, and the power of non-military means to achieve objectives exceeds the power of weapons in effectiveness.

Some label it the "Gerasimov doctrine," which is a combination of political, military, economic, social, and media means to achieve Russian strategic objectives. In the United States we would call this a whole-of-government approach.

So my question would be to any of you, and I'll start with you, Mr. Watts, if possible: Is Russia's meddling in our 2016 election proof that the United States is dealing with a nation that is acting in its own warlike manner?

Mr. WATTS. Yes. Would you like me to comment on some of the things we can do?

Senator MANCHIN. Please.

Mr. WATTS. There are seven or eight things we could do immediately that are not very complicated.

Senator MANCHIN. My desk is not going to save me this time, right?

Mr. WATTS. No. And I'll tell you right now, I'm going to walk out of here today, I'm going to be cyber-attacked, I'm going to be discredited by trolls. My biggest fear isn't being on Putin's hit list or psychological warfare targeting. I've been doing that for two years. My biggest concern right now is I don't know what the American stance is on Russia and who's going to take care of me.

After years in the Army and the FBI, working in the intel communities today, I'm going to walk out of here and ain't nobody going to be covering my back. I'm going to be on my own. So that's very disconcerting. I think that speaks to what we need to do.

One, in terms of falsehoods, we need to do two things. We need a State Department and a DHS website that immediately refutes when falsehoods are put out. These seem silly when they come out. Incirlik terrorist attack, for example. But the quicker they're refuted, the faster they die on social media. We caught the Incirlik attack because it was refuted quickly. When the Russians fake it, it gets exposed. If it goes on too long, it gets in the mainstream media and it runs out of control.

The other part is the FBI. They're doing a great job in terms of investigating hacking, but the hacking powers influence. Whenever there's a hack we should immediately go in and look at what was stolen and figure out what is the anticipated smear campaign discrediting, how is this going to be weaponized in influence.

The next one I think is super-important, which is educating U.S. businesses. Treasury and Commerce right now need to be doing awareness campaigns. Their companies suffer smear campaigns from foreign countries right now which change their stock prices. Their employees are in social media and are being picked off through social engineering and hacked.

The other part really is in the private sector and the public sector that we need to look at. Mainstream media companies, we need to be working with them. What if they boycotted WikiLeaks collectively? What if they all didn't race to publish too quickly? If the damaging, stolen information that is misconstrued oftentimes, doesn't get into the mainstream media, if all of them block it out, Russia's influence dies on the vine.

The last thing I think is the social media companies. Whether we like it or not, social media has become the news provider for almost all Americans. Our preferences shape what we see and our friends share stuff with us and it reinforces our views. So I think that for them, they're worried about these state-sponsored groups in their systems and how it's going to erode their company.

Senator MANCHIN. Dr. Godson, I'd like to ask you, if possible, when the Iron Curtain fell and Russia fell out of the world power status, superpower status I might say, how long was that hiatus? And when it came back, did it come back with a vengeance because of Putin's leadership and determination not to be shelved?

Dr. GODSON. I wish we had more information about this. Some areas we know a lot and in some areas——

Senator MANCHIN. Well, did you see basically a drop-off during the 1990s?

Dr. GODSON. We do see a bit of a drop-off, yes. However, the training, the development of cadre, continues. The hierarchy wasn't well established in terms of controlling all the various——

Senator MANCHIN. Was it under Putin basically all this came back? Can anybody say that?

Dr. Rumer.

Dr. RUMER. Yes, sir. In the 1990s Russia was flat on its back. It just didn't have the resources and a lot of the capital in this area that it had accumulated basically fell apart. I think they were very, very frustrated during the Balkan wars when they really couldn't counter what they saw as our information domination of the airwaves. So in the early 2000s when their economy came back, the apparatus came back with it, too.

Could I just add one——

Senator MANCHIN. Could I just ask one thing, because my time is running down here? Under Putin do you believe it's impossible to build a relationship to basically bring this back into some type of civility or order? Or is he just absolutely totally committed in the direction he's been going and will continue to go no matter what?

Dr. GODSON. Can I just add in answer to that?

Senator MANCHIN. Quickly.

Dr. GODSON. It depends on what the costs are. In other words, what are we going to do in response?

Senator MANCHIN. He only reacts to power out of power.

Dr. GODSON. Beg your pardon?

Senator MANCHIN. He only reacts back out of strength, if we have strength.

Dr. GODSON. Most of us react to power and strength, too. But in this case we don't yet have enough information. The committee and the study that you're doing is very important for us, not just scholars studying this subject. It's very important because we can't really answer the question about why this time and why it's successful. We're not even sure what happened here. We have the ICA statement of January.

But I just sort of want to put in a note of caution here. We sometimes in the United States think we know things and we have our sort of group-think and we all express certain views. And then we find out that later on maybe the sources of our evidence, the way we put the evidence together, didn't really make as much sense as we thought it did at the time.

Now, we've had that in our recent experience in the 1990s and 2002 and 2003, and so on. I would just say we need a little bit of caution here to be able to know exactly what happened. There's so much information out, real and false and a mixture.

Senator MANCHIN. I want to thank you so much. I'm really exceeding my time. They've been so kind to me. But thank you.

Chairman BURR. Senator Cotton.

Senator COTTON. Thank you, gentlemen, for your appearance this morning.

I want to return to the topic Senator Lankford broached, which is why Vladimir Putin and Russia's leaders thought they could get away with such a brazen set of actions last year, and doing so in a, quote, "noisy" fashion, as Director Comey testified last week. Dr. Godson, I'd like to hear your point of view on this.

Specifically, I'd like to hear your thoughts about the context in which Vladimir Putin did this in 2015 and 2016. In the previous eight years, Russia had invaded Georgia, it had invaded and seized Crimea, its rebels had been supported in Eastern Ukraine to occupy the Donbas, they'd been provided missiles and shot a civilian aircraft out of the sky. Russia had repeatedly violated the INF Treaty.

The Obama Administration had come into office proclaiming a reset and in 2012 Barack Obama mocked his opponent for claiming that Russia was our number one foe and promised Dmitry Medvedev that more could be done after the election when he had more flexibility.

Would that series of events have emboldened Vladimir Putin to think he might be able to get away with such a noisy intrusion into our political system?

Dr. GODSON. I would suggest that you're right. I think that this does not help in restraining Russian interest in expanding in the near abroad and as far abroad as they can. So that the train of actions you described there didn't exactly persuade him that we would take his intervening in other matters, such as elections, seriously.

So it's going to take, I think, some time and some activity by the United States, some important activity, to be able to establish our reputation in this arena. I know it's beyond the gist of the arena for the Intelligence Committee, but intelligence can play a major role in this. But I think that this is a whole-of-government, this is a policy issue, and it's more than intelligence.

But I would hope, though, that we are in fact gaining the kinds of information we need to have an informed judgment about what you are asking about, in other words was he tempted by our lack of action? I hope, I presume, that the intelligence community has a tasking that identifies the Soviet responses and their perceptions and that if we don't have such a tasking on this subject then we won't be in a very good position to act.

But I think in general, yes, I agree with the point you're making. I think the evidence is strong, but we need stronger information, too, to give us better judgment on this kind of issue.

Senator COTTON. Dr. Rumer, I don't think you've had a chance to opine on this question yet.

Dr. RUMER. Thank you, sir. I believe that the biggest factor in Putin's decision to pursue this aggressive line of intervention in our domestic politics has been the realization on their part, as Mr. Watts suggested, that this is a very lucrative environment in which they can achieve a lot with even a remotely plausible claim of deniability. So I think they just took advantage of the environment here.

Senator COTTON. Mr. Watts.

Mr. WATTS. Yes, I'd like to add to what I said before. One, I don't think they thought their hand was going to be exposed as much as it is today. I think they thought they could do it in a more subtle fashion. So my belief is right now in Russia they're probably trying to figure out, how do I manage this situation now where I have extended myself?

But the overriding issue with why Russia did this to the United States and does it now to Europe is we are weak. We do not respond. We have no organized response as a country or even a policy toward Russia right now. So I think until we set the boundaries about how we are going to either push forward with them, they're going to move as far as they can push. And then when we set our policy positions, which we don't have right now, they'll move in kind based on whatever that is.

Senator COTTON. I have one final question about active measures. Dr. Godson, you talked in your testimony or in your opening statement about some of the history of Russian active measures. It's been going on for a long time. Bob Gates, former Director of the CIA and Secretary of Defense, wrote in his first memoir, "From the Shadows," about Russia's campaign against the NATO deployment of intermediate-range nuclear forces in Europe in 1983, quote:

"During the period, the Soviets mounted a massive covert action operation aimed at thwarting INF deployments by NATO. We at the CIA devoted tremendous resources and effort at the time to uncovering this Soviet covert campaign." End quote.

The United States is currently undergoing a long-delayed, deeply needed nuclear modernization campaign, upgrading our bombers, our dual-capable aircraft, our ground-based missiles, our long-range standoff cruise missile, and our submarine capability as well.

Do you believe there is any chance that Russia is not currently engaged in an active measures campaign to try to thwart that modernization effort in the United States?

Dr. GODSON. No, I think you're right. I think you're right. I do believe almost certainly that they are. If not already engaged in it, they will be.

Senator COTTON. Because that is simply what Russia does.

Dr. GODSON. That is simply what this particular leadership, successors to the previous generation, yes, I believe, do. I don't think it's inevitable Russians will do this, but I think these fellows will do it.

Senator COTTON. I apologize, gentlemen. My time has expired.

Chairman BURR. Senator King.

Senator KING. Thank you, Mr. Chair.

Just to sort of sum up what I've heard this morning: Number one, it appears that we're engaged in a new form of aggression, if not war, that the Soviet Union and now Russia has been utilizing for many years, but is now taking it to a much higher level. It strikes me that Vladimir Putin is playing a weak hand very well.

A couple of questions, very, very short. I would say that what we've seen and what you've told us this morning is that what we saw in the 2016 election is absolutely consistent with prior Russian practice and current Russian practice in other parts of Europe and the world. Is that correct, Mr. Watts?

Mr. WATTS. Yes, it's still going on today.

Senator KING. Secondly, is it your opinion that this is going to continue? In other words, 2016 is not a one-off?

Mr. WATTS. No. I mean, they're going to continue until something meets their challenge, and right now there's nothing meeting their challenge. Any European effort I've seen is very small in comparison.

Senator KING. Mr. Rumer, would you say that, Dr. Rumer, that Putin is a Democrat, a Republican, or an opportunist?

Dr. RUMER. I think he's an opportunist. And even if we counter this or when we counter his efforts, he will continue anyway. It's going to be a dynamic, not a sort of static situation where we deploy countermeasures and it stops. He will keep going on it.

Senator KING. I think it's very important, though, that we realize that he is neither a Democrat nor a Republican, because it means that everybody on this dais and everybody in political life in America regardless of their party is at risk. In 2016 it happened to tilt because of his interest toward the political candidate of the Republican Party. But it could very well be the opposite in 2020 or 2022.

Mr. Watts, you're nodding, but we can't record that.

Mr. WATTS. Yes, they will shift to whichever one supports or is most amenable to their foreign policy position or who they think is weak for manipulation. They will go with whichever one it is.

Senator KING. And one thing that was mentioned today somewhat briefly, but it came up in some of the questions, is not only did they hack the Democratic National Committee and misinformation and disinformation and all of that, but they also pushed and probed into our State election systems in a number of states. Apparently the information that we have thus far is it didn't work. But they tried.

Mr. Watts, would you agree that they weren't trying for fun? This wasn't entertainment; they were looking for a place to make changes in election results?

Mr. WATTS. What no one's talking about is the information nukes that Russia sits on right now because they hacked 3,000 to 4,000 people. I think this afternoon you're going to hear on the cyber more technical side, this hacking was pervasive. We've focused on the DNC. I've been targeted. Some other people have been targeted that I know.

They have our information, so any time anyone rises up that they choose against, whether it's Republican or a Democrat, Congress or Executive Branch or a State official, they've got the ability to do the same thing they just did over the past year.

Senator KING. I want to touch on that in a minute, but I do want—do you believe that they will try again to compromise State-level election voting machines, registration rolls?

Mr. WATTS. They could.

Senator KING. They tried this time.

Mr. WATTS. I don't think it's about breaking into the election machines. The goal is to create the perception that the vote may not be authentic. So that's why it's smart to target voter rolls, because just the act of hitting a voter roll doesn't change the vote, but then you can run an influence story that says there's voter fraud in the United States, that the election is rigged, that the count wasn't accurate, and you can gain traction with it. It's a pinprick perception that they're trying to create.

Senator KING. You have mentioned several times, and I think the Russian term is, "kompromat." I think it's interesting that they have a Russian term which is compromising information. This is active in the sense that not only can they take things off your computer, they can put things on your computer that will compromise you. I think that should send a shudder through all Americans, that this isn't only taking—you can be very careful in your emails, but something can show up on your computer that's fake and you could be in a lot of trouble.

This is one of their techniques, is it not?

Mr. WATTS. Yes. Americans should look to Europe, where this has happened quite a bit more frequently.

Senator KING. Finally, we talked a bit about—you talked a bit about defenses. I think this is something that our committee in its report is going to have to look at. Cyber strategy is one. We have no cyber strategy in this country. There's no knowledge around the world of how we will react to a cyber attack, and I think that's part of what we have to do.

Digital literacy, and that is people understanding the limitations of what they have on the internet. My wife has a sign in our kitchen that says "The problem with quotes on the internet is you can't determine whether they're authentic. Abraham Lincoln." We have to educate our people that they can't believe everything that they read on the internet, and part of that is I think your very creative suggestion of a kind of Snopes, expanded Snopes, to check the validity, so people at least know, okay, there's some likelihood that

that is untrue. And finally, public awareness, which is what this hearing is all about.

Thank you, Mr. Chairman. I appreciate it.

Chairman BURR. Thank you, Senator King.

Senator Cornyn.

Senator CORNYN. Mr. Chairman, let me start by complimenting you and the Vice Chairman again for your leadership. This is really important. I saw Senator Lankford and Senator——

Chairman BURR. King.

Senator CORNYN [continuing]. King, thank you—I had a blank—on TV this morning talking about why this was so important to our country and why it's so important we have a bipartisan investigation and follow the facts wherever they may lead.

Mr. Watts, let me follow up on some of what Senator King was alluding to. I remember, of course, it wasn't that long ago where the Office of Personnel Management was hacked and 21 million records, personnel records, were stolen of U.S. Government workers. Of that, about 5 million plus fingerprints included.

I'm also remembering that a few years ago there was a story—I think it was in 2016—a story about the tactics that Putin uses to discredit political opponents in Russia and elsewhere. The New York Times story I pulled up said: "Foes of Russia say child pornography is planted to ruin them." The sort of tactics that are being used both domestically and internationally against foes of the Putin administration, the sort of hacks, the cyber attacks and the access to personnel records, the computers of all of us—all of these render us susceptible to this sort of influence campaigns, correct?

Mr. WATTS. Yes. Americans need to understand that anything they do on the computer can be public at some point.

Senator CORNYN. And just because it appears on the computer doesn't necessarily mean it's true?

Mr. WATTS. Correct. Fact and fiction have been wildly blurred over the past few years.

Senator CORNYN. Regarding the last election and Putin's active measures effort, is it reasonable to conclude that any efforts made to weaken the candidacy of Hillary Clinton by doing damage to her reputation, credibility, and political standing would have been a desirable outcome for Russia even if she were elected President?

Mr. WATTS. Yes. The goal was either to get your candidate elected that you approve of or to just totally discredit and undermine the mandate of whoever does win should it be your opponent.

Senator CORNYN. Mr. Rumer.

Dr. RUMER. Yes, sir, I agree.

Senator CORNYN. So do we have any reason to believe that Putin knew more than the pundits and pollsters did here in America about the outcome of the election before it occurred?

Mr. WATTS. No.

Senator CORNYN. The electoral result is what I'm referring to. I didn't think so.

Dr. Godson, you mentioned earlier, and I believe several of you alluded to this—about a strategic approach to countermeasures. Would you briefly describe what some of those might be? And I would like to have a more extended conversation at some point about what each of you would recommend for the United States

Government to do to engage in a strategic approach of counter-measures to this sort of campaign.

Dr. Godson.

Dr. GODSON. Well, we have had a historical precedent for developing that strategic approach. This is actually what happened in the Reagan years, that we decided that there was a major active measures offensive, much higher than people had expected, and we had to respond. So there were a couple of things that were done then which seemed to be quite effective and I would recommend we take those things that worked and put them into our strategic approach.

Senator CORNYN. Could you give us a few examples?

Dr. GODSON. Yes. One is what we're sort of starting to do now and what you're starting to do, is educating the American and other populations about the threat of active measures and the price one can pay for successful active measures, so that when they know and hear about it they're not taken by it, it doesn't influence them. One is education.

A second capability that we would need would be ways of reducing the effectiveness of the active measures: warning, anticipating, education, and then what can be done to reduce the effectiveness of the active measures? One of the things that worked in the past was exposing the perpetrators of the active measures, preferably in real time, but anyway exposure.

Senator CORNYN. As Mr. Watts pointed out, the advent of social media and the use of social media to move fake stories around the internet and to get mainstream media to pay attention to them, and without authenticating the source of the information, then repeating it, successfully amplifying that message, strikes me as a huge challenge.

All of us have run for elections and had to deal with the changes in the way we communicate with each other. It is a huge challenge. I don't know how we get to the bottom of this and find some site, some trusted site, government or otherwise, that says this is the truth, this is not the truth, don't believe what you're being told.

Dr. GODSON. Senator, we did have some good experience with it. We didn't have the machines. They didn't have those capabilities, the mechanical capabilities. But we still were able to discredit a lot of their active measures and the apparatus, and so it was effective for a while.

The third part of this, though, really the hard part, is what kind of whole-of-government responses are we going to develop to actually deal with the problem? We sort of have to come to grips with this. As I said, this may not be the only committee that has to deal with this. But we have to say, what are we willing to tolerate? Are there any red lines for us, that if they go over this line then there will be these kinds of responses?

We developed this kind of deterrence policy. We have rules of the road in deterrence so both sides don't get too close to each other on the nuclear weapons issues. But we're going to have to start to figure out what it is we're going to do and what we're going to accept and what we're going to tolerate and what kinds of responses we're going to have, not just once in a while, but consistently in this arena. I thank you for the question.

Senator CORNYN. Thank you.

Thank you, Mr. Chairman.

Chairman BURR. Senator Harris.

Senator HARRIS. Thank you, and I want to thank the Chairman and Vice Chairman for this open hearing. As this committee conducts its investigation into Russia's interference with our 2016 United States election, the American people need to fully understand the threat that we face and what we must do to protect ourselves in the future.

Let's all be clear about what happened. We know, as has already been determined by the CIA, the FBI, and the NSA, a foreign country, Russia, attacked the heart of our democracy, an American election for the President of the United States. And they can and will do so again if we do not act urgently.

We must get to the bottom of this. We must be thorough. We must proceed with urgency. And we must be transparent. That is vital to protect the public's trust in us and it's what the American people deserve. I know we can do so while protecting classified sources and material items that must remain classified in order to protect our national security, the sources of our intelligence, and the sensitive methods by which we collect it.

This hearing is a first step to understand Russia's interference, but it cannot end here. We must build on today's hearing with future open hearings as much as possible. I strongly believe an informed public is one of our best weapons against future attacks.

That being said, I have a question for all of you, and I'll start with Mr. Watts. Earlier this week, former Vice President Cheney said Russia's interference in our election should be considered an act of war. Assuming this was an act of war, Russia is investing in cyber weapons and cyber soldiers, which we call trolls, while we continue to invest in conventional weapons. As we invest in fighter jets and aircraft carriers, Russia is investing in state-run media from which it can push out fake news.

As we consider investing more than $600 billion in our defense budget, Russia has approximately one-tenth of that amount in their budget and is developing its cyber warfare capabilities. I strongly believe cyber may be the new frontier of war.

So my question to you is: Was this an act of war and are we prepared for this new form of warfare? And equally important, given the everyday challenges of Americans in their everyday lives, why should they be concerned about this?

Mr. WATTS. On the first part, an act of war, on the scale of warfare, it's not kinetic, but it's definitely part of the Cold War system that we knew 20, 30 years ago. Americans should be concerned because right now a foreign country, whether they realize it or not, is pitting them against their neighbor, other political parties, ramping up divisions based on things that aren't true.

They're trying to break down the trust they have in you as a Senator, the Congress, the legislature, the court system. They're trying to break down all faith in those institutions. And if they can do that, if Americans don't believe that their vote counts, they're not going to show up to participate in democracy. If they don't believe that what they're doing is part of a government system that actually represents them, they're not going to go to jury duty. If they don't believe in those institutions, everything breaks down, and when that breakdown occurs we are focusing internally and Russia is focused externally, achieving their goals.

In terms of investments, part of the reason we don't invest well in cyber and we don't invest in information is because we're not buying big pieces of equipment. If you can't buy a big piece of equipment, then it's really hard to invest your dollars. We need to invest in people. The reason Russians win in cyber and information space is they have great propagandists and they have the best hackers that are out there, that they can either enlist because they're criminals and sort of bring them under the umbrella or train themselves.

We, on the other hand, worry a lot about who we're going to bring into the cyber field because they might have smoked weed one day or they can't pass the security clearance or they didn't get a score on their ASVAB, but there's millions, I mean millions, of talented Americans out there that can support these roles inside our government. We need to invest in humans moving forward in this space.

It's hard to get Americans to understand that or even the Department of Defense, because you're talking about cyber and computers and so you think of tech. But the truth is that tech only works if you've got the smartest brains behind it. We do, but we don't put them against our fight.

Senator HARRIS. Thank you.

Dr. Rumer.

Dr. RUMER. I think we should be careful using terms such as "an act of war." It's definitely the continuation of warfare by other means, but when you declare something to be an act of war it calls for certain responses that we may not be ready to take on.

I do agree with Mr. Watts on the need to be much more creative, much more resourceful, in the way we approach the question of, quote, "cyber warfare." I again would caution that the Russians have a very different standard here in using their offensive tools than we use in using our cyber tools with a great deal of responsibility, and I think we should be very careful not to cross certain lines.

We should, however, be using the tools that are available to us and platforms that are available to us just from a somewhat different domain. I think that our own spokesmen, our own information projected and delivered from our platforms, should be the gold standard of accuracy and objectivity. So from that standpoint, let me just say that we're not using, for example, the platform of the State Department effectively. The practice of not sustaining our regular briefings for the media for the world is something that only hurts our interests.

Senator HARRIS. Thank you.

Dr. GODSON. I agree with my colleagues, so I won't repeat the same conclusions they reached. I would, though, like to introduce the idea that cyber is now important. Cyber wasn't considered so important 20 years ago, now considered important. But there are other technologies coming on board now. Some are visible to us. Some, they're not very salient; they haven't risen above the horizon.

There are a whole number of technologies that are not internet-dependent. As we look at active measures now and into the future, I would think that would be on the agenda. I'll give you just one example—virtual reality. Anybody who can set up the reality is going to have a very decided advantage in politics and other areas.

So as we are looking at cyber—and you are going to have this hearing and other studies on this—I would say just that we should be broadening the concept of technologies that are going to be available, coming online, and it would be extremely unlikely that the Russians would ignore those technologies. So maybe that would be something to add to the already busy agenda that you have.

Thank you.

Senator HARRIS. Thank you.

Chairman BURR. Thank you, Senator.

Thank you to all of our witnesses. All the questions have been asked except for mine. So let me, if I could, spend just a couple of minutes. I agree with you, Dr. Godson, the ability to impersonate online is the next phase that we will go through. I think it's safe to say we don't have our best and brightest yet focused on that. We're still trying to triage what happened to us versus to be creative and look forward and say what could happen.

Mr. Watts, I heard you talk about intent and specifically the intent of the Russians and their effectiveness and how pre-planning played a large part of the 2016 effort. Here's my disconnect, is that when you—at least on the surface, as we've gotten into the investigation, as you look at the emails that were captured either out of the DNC or out of the Podesta account that were then the source of Russia's effort through WikiLeaks to publicly lay this out, that seemed to be an average, ordinary Russian fishing expedition, that we captured maybe 3,000 efforts at the same period in time.

So are you suggesting that they had an effort to mess with the elections and just happened to be lucky enough to stumble across a volume of emails?

Mr. WATTS. They go widespread. Whatever the best nuggets that come out of that is what they run with. They hit a gold mine and they were able to successfully find the ammunition they wanted. What you see in other cases is they do compromise other accounts—I'm not going to talk about them; I don't want to amplify them—but they're less successful. You know, we'll hear a dump and you'll be like, oh, this isn't really anything other than what I expected a politician to say.

So they hit a whale whenever they went fishing. But I would also say that somewhere in their cache right now there is tremendous amounts of information laying around they can weaponize against other Americans.

Chairman BURR. We would agree with you on that.

Very quickly, as you sort of summarized how fake news and how coordinated social media efforts push stories to the top ten and they get picked up automatically, what is the takeaway for U.S. media outlets from what you just said?

Mr. WATTS. They have to improve their editorial processes and they also have to take a step back from the "I gotta get it out first" competitive environment. Part of the reason this Russian system works is every outlet races to get the story out first. When they do that, they put themselves at risk to fall for these sorts of schemes. Until they improve that or until they collectively, we have some sort of standard that either the public or the media holds itself to, we're going to keep seeing them fall for these campaigns, whether it's Russia, by the way, or others. You're going to see many other nations take this on now that the playbook's been thrown out there.

Chairman BURR. Dr. Rumer, would you like to take the opportunity to address in greater detail what the Russians are doing in the French and German elections?

Dr. RUMER. Well, sir, there's a wide effort in the German election to build up the far-right party, Alternative for Germany, AfG, to use them as sort of a credible challenger to Chancellor Angela Merkel. There are countless stories that are being spread through fake news sites and media about the failures of Chancellor Merkel. They, as others have pointed out, have exploited the story about the girl that was not raped, but to again discredit her in the eyes of the general public so as to point out her failure to protect Germany against the flood of refugees. That's one of their major policy initiatives that she took when the Syria crisis broke out.

In the French election, we just saw something that really was staggering and that is President Putin hosted in the Kremlin the leading far-right candidate and, almost with a smirk, said that: "We don't interfere in French elections, but we have the right to engage any candidate in the public domain in that contest."

Also, Russian disinformation sources have spread malicious stories about one of the leading candidates, Emmanuel Macron, about his personal life.

Chairman BURR. For the first time, we're really beginning to see an effort to build up and to absolutely destroy the character of others, having a double impact potentially on the outcome of the election?

Dr. RUMER. Yes, sir.

Chairman BURR. Dr. Godson, just quickly, how did we respond differently when we overcame these active measures by Russians pre-1980? And is there a lesson for us to learn from that in our actions now?

Dr. GODSON. I think there are a number of lessons, but one was this exposure business, that we learned how to put out information to the public domain that not only was relevant for Americans, but for foreigners. And we briefed that and we developed teams that could go out and talk about these things and so neutralize a lot.

That was one of the methods that we could replicate. A second was support to elements abroad who are trying to maintain the democratic process. We developed some capabilities to do that. We still have some. One of the outstanding examples is the National Endowment for Democracy—bipartisan, able to do quite a lot, but it also limited in various ways. So one could look back to see how we were able to do this in different ways abroad that had an effect in the past. It's not that expensive financially and those methods are available.

Chairman BURR. Thank you.

Mr. Watts, just very briefly, has anybody taken you up on your list of recommendations?

Mr. WATTS. No.

Chairman BURR. That did not go unnoticed by the committee. I want you to know that. Nor did the comment that there was agreement on at the table, that America's response to date has been woefully short of what it should be; if anything, it should be interpreted, and probably was interpreted, by the Russians that they can double down and in fact do it unscathed.

So Mr. Watts, we heard you when you said fact and fiction had become wildly blurred. Let me just assure you that this committee's mission every day is to do the oversight on the intelligence community, 17 agencies, that assures the American people we do everything within the letter of the law. We first assure that to 85 other members of the Senate. So when it came time for a look inside what Russia active measures did and what our response was and how our intelligence community came to the assessments that they did, this fell right in our wheelhouse.

This is what our professional staff does on a daily basis. This is a little more granular than what we do. It will take some time and it means triaging a tremendous amount of documents.

But I also heard from all three of you that if there was ever a time to get it right, it's now. We have methodically built a process that builds a foundation of fact, to build an investigation on that foundation that can hopefully come to a bipartisan finding where the conclusions are matched with the facts that we find.

In some cases, as all three of you know, that might be intelligence product that can't be made public. But in every place that we can, I have pledged to the Vice Chairman and he has pledged to his members and I have pledged to mine, where we can make it public so that the American people understand it and feel that this has been credible and thorough and that the conclusions are valid, we're going to try to do that.

But I also believe that the American people expect us to protect sources and methods. They expect us to work with the intelligence community in a way that strengthens what they do and how they do it, not by sharing that with everybody, but by certifying that they're doing it within the letter of the law to keep America safe.

I look at this investigation as one extension of that and it's to once again certify to the American people what we've done has been thorough, to hopefully provide some actionable conclusions for this Administration, and to look back on the work that we do and believe that in 2018 and 2020 we're going to be less concerned with Russia's involvement in our elections and that the United States of America should, like we do on terrorism, work with any country in the world that might be the target of an aggressor like Vladimir Putin.

So I'm grateful to you for what you've contributed to our investigation.

This hearing is now adjourned.

[Whereupon, at 12:31 p.m., the hearing was adjourned.]